A good guide book is essential for every traveller going somewhere new for a holiday. *Heaven: A Guide* is a fact-packed, no nonsense guide book that tells you everything you will ever need to know about Heaven – how to get there, what to do there and how to make the most of the holiday of a lifetime!

Have you ever wondered about travel arrangements – should we book in advance? Is there a stand-by service for last minute departures? For those with weak stomachs is air turbulence likely with out-of-body flights? Is there in-flight entertainment? Is a meal provided or should we grab a snack beforehand in the departure lounge? *Heaven: A Guide* answers all these questions and more. Information on entry regulations, interrogations by border guards or immigration officers, the polite form of address to St. Peter will all ensure that when you arrive there is no danger of repatriation, refusal of entry or any of those hellish delays.

Meeting you-know-who could be a nerve-racking experience if you had no advice on how to behave and what to say. Having briefed yourself properly with the information given in these pages, meeting your maker will be a once in a lifetime experience.

HEAVEN

A GUIDE

Compiled by
Angela Devine and Rory Fellowes

International Editors:
Said Irafta, Gottfried Himmel and Ivan Tchellikle

London
UNWIN PAPERBACKS
Boston Sydney

First published in Great Britain by Unwin Paperbacks 1985

UNWIN® PAPERBACKS
40 Museum Street, London, WC1A 1LU, UK

Unwin Paperbacks
Park Lane, Hemel Hempstead, Herts HP2 4TE, UK

George Allen & Unwin Australia Pty Ltd.,
8 Napier Street, North Sydney, NSW 2060, Australia

Unwin Paperbacks with the
Port Nicholson Press
PO Box 11-838 Wellington, New Zealand

British Library Cataloguing in Publication Data

Heaven: a guide.
828′.91407 PR6054.E8/
ISBN 0-04-827084-9

Set in 10 on 11 point Palatino by V & M Graphics Ltd, Aylesbury, Bucks
and printed in Great Britain by Cox and Wyman, Reading

CONTENTS

HEAVEN

Terra lactis mellisque

INTRODUCTION

The mystery of unknown lands, the thrill of discovering new worlds, the taste of another life that few of us even dream of – Heaven offers this and much, much more to the world-weary and earth-spent.

Heaven isn't just the fulfilment of a lifetime's ambition; it's the ultimate destination for every discerning traveller. Yet Heaven's attractions are not simple to define. Balmy zephyrs wafting on ethereal shores, the sweet music of local harpists drifting through Arcadian groves, the absence of telephones and pollution, these are some of the immediate delights. But Heaven has other, subtler, deeper attractions lying beneath its pure, untarnished surface. The landscape itself presents the visitor with the gift of leisure – for time has no part here – and space; a vast unending spaciousness that knows no bounds and which for some reason seems so much bigger than anywhere you've been before.

There may be times when the visitor feels lost in Heaven. The journey itself is a traumatic experience, especially if you 'walk the long road' alone. There are those who have returned unsettled from their experiences, disillusioned with the life they have found, perhaps – unprepared and ill-equipped for it more likely. For the journey to Heaven is like no other and the haven that welcomes the weary traveller is a world away from the one left behind. In brief, to make the most of Heaven and all that it offers you need an informative and comprehensive guide, which we hope the following pages will provide.

Here you'll find a handy, pocket-sized companion to prepare for the journey that will change your life. There are tips on where to eat, where to stay, where to go for the best in local night-life. There's detailed information on travel, entry formalities, what to take, how to get on with the locals and how to get away from the crowds. And there are hints aimed at the more adventurous that should open unimagined horizons to those prepared to explore them. While it's true to say that any trip to Heaven is out of the ordinary, we hope that this companion guide will help to make yours a once in a lifetime experience.

Getting to HEAVEN

EARNING YOUR PLACE

Nowadays almost everyone wants to go to Heaven – and that's not surprising because God's Kingdom is the one paradise land that fully lives up to its reputation.

And the good news is that getting to Heaven has never been easier. Once upon a time the entry conditions were tough – damned tough – but since the sharp drop in immigration that occurred in the 1960s the Almighty has seen fit to relax the rules a bit, and today, no matter what you did on Earth, provided you *meant well*, your place in Paradise is as good as guaranteed.

To be one hundred per cent certain of gaining admission you only have to keep your nose clean while you're alive (you won't get colds after you're dead) and, as a mortal, remember these important Do's and Don't's:

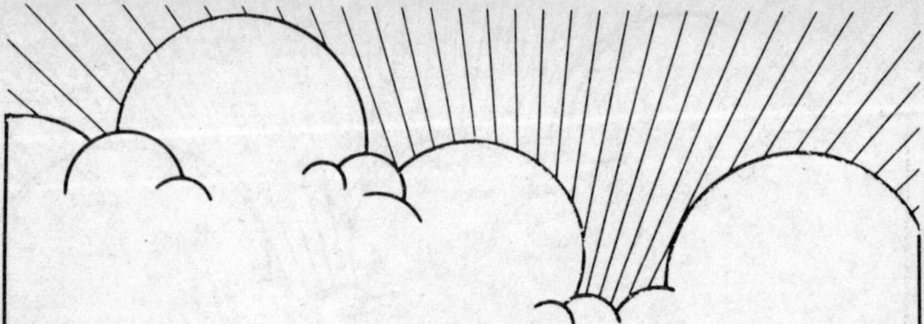

DO	DON'T
Always try to say 'please' 'thank you' and 'it's a pleasure'.	Always say '... or else!' 'What's it to you?' or 'Stuff it'.
Always try to shed a ray of kindness as you pass.	Always smirk when the dollar slumps/Manchester United lose/the neighbour's cat gets stuck in a tree.
Try to be nice to everyone you meet.	Try to be nice to everyone you meet, while telling yourself that they're a load of ...
Say your prayers every day.	Just say your prayers every time you want a favour, or the phone bill arrives.
Say 'pardon' after you break wind.	Say 'pardon!' after someone else has broken wind.
Tell the truth the whole time.	Tell the truth the whole time, if all you're going to say is what a huge nose the man next door has got.
Repent every time you do wrong.	Yell 'You'll be sorry!' every time someone else does wrong.
Go to church for a purpose.	Go to church for a purpose if that purpose is nicking the lead from the roof or lifting the Communion plate.

Other points to remember

- Anyone arriving at Heaven with a Visa marked 'Hell' in their passports may well be refused admission. The possession of two passports will not guarantee entry.

- Sudden bursts of evangelism and philanthropy immediately before departure will not necessarily impress the immigration authorities. Remember John Milton: 'They also serve who only stand and wait.'
- While it may be better to give than to receive, avoid blatant bribery at your entry point. The penalties for deception are severe. It is particularly inadvisable to offer freshly-picked apples to frontier personnel.

ADMISSION PROCEDURE – ENTRY REQUIREMENTS – CUSTOMS FORMALITIES

When you get to the Pearly Gates you will be met by St Peter, who is a brick (or a rock, depending on the translation used), and his Reception Committee. They will ask you to complete an application form for entry into Heaven (which for convenience and prior warning we have reprinted here), and they will ask you a few questions before you're allowed in.

The application form is quite straightforward, but it is impossible to predict the sorts of questions that you will be asked at the interview, or to say exactly what sort of personality or characteristics St Peter and his team most favour. This is due to the broad-based immigration policy that has been operating in Heaven since Creation. Guided by divine omnipotence this has been singularly successful in maintaining a healthy balance in the world above, while weeding out the less desirable elements of earthly society. This policy still remains a mystery until the admission interview itself. As a general rule aspiring applicants are well advised to read the admission's handbook, sold on

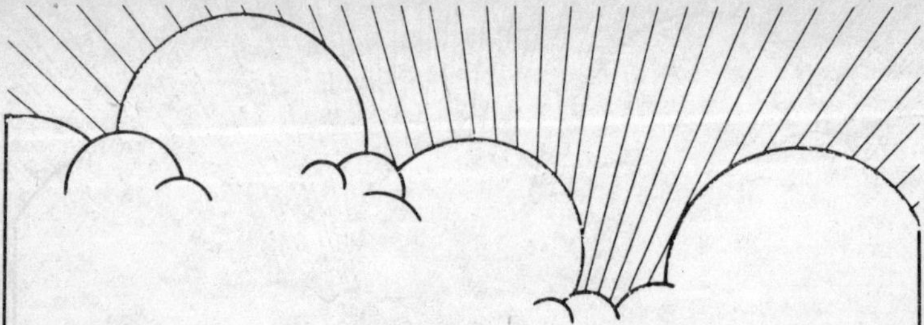

Earth as the Bible. Special note should be given to the experience of one Saul of Tarsus (later known as Paul). Incidentally, it is inadvisable to confuse this Saul with an Old Testament king of the same name.

On arrival you may well find that blondes are making the running, where the week before those with blue eyes were being let in, and the week before that those with pleasant speaking voices. Attractive, outward going personalities are frequently transparent in front of St Peter and his trained staff. As one successful applicant described it, 'When you're shooting the dice on the Lord's table, you gotta box pretty.' In short, go in prepared to bare your soul and put your trust in God. Remember: The Almighty doesn't want an empty Heaven, so the odds are in your favour.

THE UNITED KINGDOM OF HEAVEN – APPLICATION FORM FOR ENTRY AND PERMANENT RESIDENCE

Forename/Christian name (where applicable) ....
Surname .... Place and date of birth ....
Nationality .... Religion (if none tear up form) ....
Occupation on earth .... Sponsor in Heaven ....
Reason for journey .... Date of arrival ....
Means of support in Heaven (outline assets, faiths etc) ....
....
Sins/Transgressions* ....
....
(Continue overleaf. Ask gatekeeper if additional sheets are required)
(* IF NONE, WRITE 'LIAR')

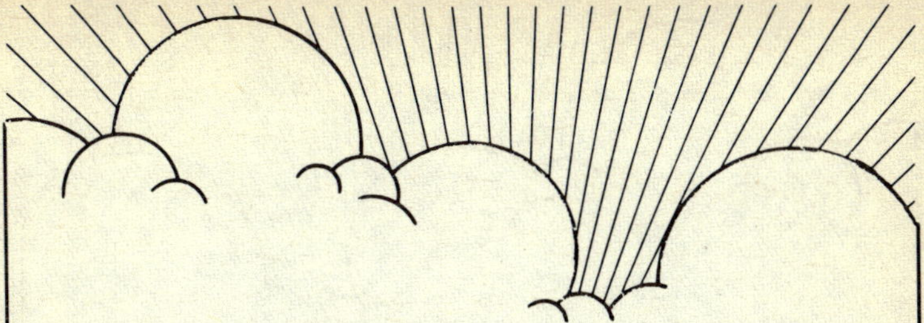

1. Have you ever visited Heaven before? ☐ Yes ☐ No
   If 'Yes' state reasons for leaving ....
   If 'No' state when you didn't visit ....
2. Are you a practising Christian? ☐ Yes ☐ No
   If 'Yes', when did you practise ....
3. Qualifications ☐ Innocence ☐ Reformed sinner ☐ Theology degree ☐ Bishop ☐ Pope ☐ List any other qualifications (Saint, Martyr etc) in Holy Order ....
4. Accomplishments: Harp playing ☐ Ministering ☐ Choir practice ☐
5. Colour of hair .... (Please attach sample)
6. Colour of eyes Left Right Middle
7. Colour of skin .... (Ask a friend to help)
8. Do you hold a current driving licence Yes No
9. Are you prepared to grow wings?
   - ☐ Yes
   - ☐ No
   - ☐ Undecided
   - ☐ Because it gives good all round visibility
   - ☐ Yes, on wet roads
   - ☐ Robert Redford
   - ☐ 1956 – Twice
   - ☐ Flora Margarine
   - ☐ Celtic
10. Complete the following phrase in less than 36 chapters:
    I would like to visit Heaven because ....

Notes

a All fees must be paid in advance. Penance, confession, fasting, and other terms available on request.

b BUSINESS AND TRANSIT VISAS ARE NO LONGER OBTAINABLE IN HEAVEN.

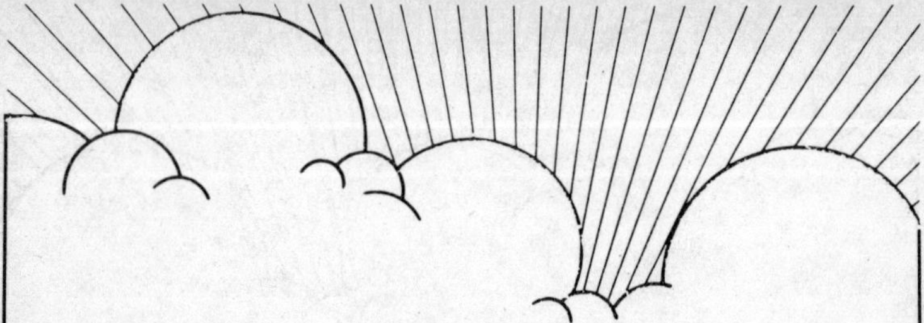

THE JOURNEY

The journey to Heaven is unique. It is the simplest journey to make, yet it's the one we knew least about. It's literally out of this world. Travelling to Heaven will be unlike any other experience you've ever had before.

Only the very self-possessed traveller has made all the necessary preparations before departure. Most visitors seem far more concerned with tying up loose ends on Earth, making sure that the final life insurance policy has been paid up and that the will has been signed, though in the last case there are usually others around to assist with making the will legal.

Assuming that you've made a clean breast of things before you leave, there shouldn't be any need to panic about getting your story right on arrival. The great advantage of telling the truth is that you don't have to remember what you said the last time. You won't need to burden yourself with the usual holiday paraphernalia either. Heaven has a strictly egalitarian society, so you can leave your flashy cameras and rhinestones behind. Visitors quickly adapt to wearing the simple local costume, which is perfectly suited to the climate and informality of the other world. Indeed, your only requirements are a pure heart and a facility to amuse yourself indefinitely. The experienced traveller travels light and your aim should be to take nothing more into Heaven than you brought into Earth.

The simplicity of travelling to Heaven is the direct result of the surprising organisation involved. In these days of multi-tiered fare structures and intricate international timetables, it's refreshing to find a journey where even the time of departure is taken out of the traveller's hands.

The simplicity of the journey has swept away the need for advance booking, route selection, airport taxes, baggage-handlers' go-slows, in-flight entertainments, in-flight meals and duty-free goods. The emphasis has been on straightforward passenger conveyance for longer than most of us can remember. And the result is a fast, efficient no-nonsense, door-to-door service that cuts out the frills and gives the traveller exactly what he, or she wants – getting the journey over and done with as fast as possible.

After the strain and tension of those last minute farewells most travellers relish the peace and silent efficiency of their skyward journey. As the Bible tells us, we step from life onto the stairway and take off for the clouds. It should be pointed out, though, that increased traffic and the desire to make constant improvements have led the authorities to introduce a staircase that befits the ultimate kingdom – an escalator.

This is no ordinary escalator. It's magnificence and scale almost defy description. From its base the traveller stares up the hypnotic curves of the disappearing spiral until it bores into the clouds and disappears from sight. Yet in spite of its immense size, the journey to Heaven is remarkable in being free from cases of travel sickness, caused either by the altitude, or the in-flight food.

The journey to Heaven is a timeless sensation. The traveller simply steps onto his or her step on the escalator and is whirled aloft. Most find that the initial thrill of peering down at passing clouds, and later at the stars, is quickly replaced by a growing sense of monotony. But this is part of the gradual process of acclimatisation to what is and always will be Heaven. As we mentioned earlier, Heaven takes some getting used to. As you peer above the

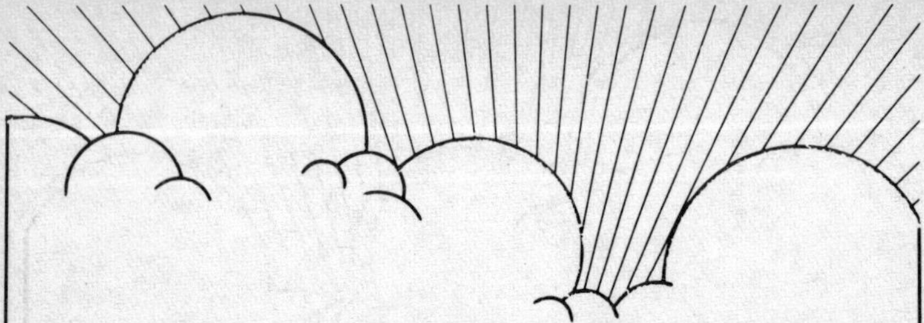

safety-rails, or look down below your feet you can see for ever and ever. Ah men! How foolish are we for ever searching for the finite. Here at last is the end to our life-long quest. Here as you move imperceptibly from one life to the next Hamlet's 'fardels' slip from your shoulders and Macbeth's 'innocent sleep' begins to quiet your restless spirit. (This sleep has been given the name of 'cloud-lag' in popular parlance, though this is a term that is seldom used in Heaven itself.)

The map below shows the itinerary. We suggest that you familiarise yourself with it before your departure, whenever that may be.

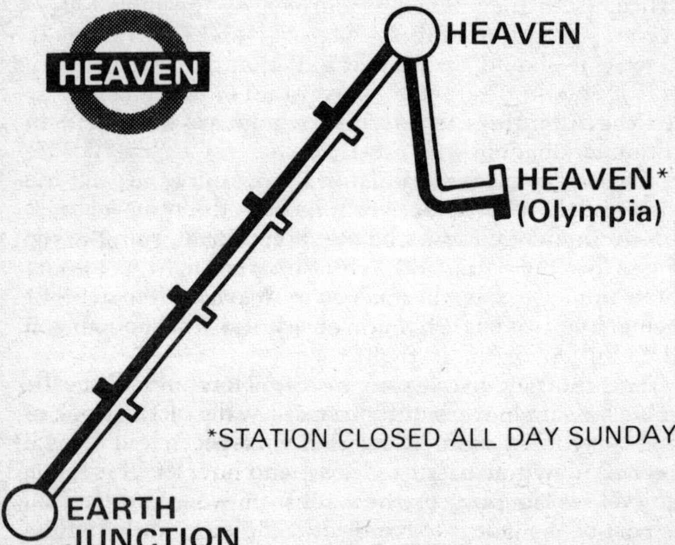

(Map supplied by courtesy of the Stairway to Heaven Mass Transport Authority – SHMTA)

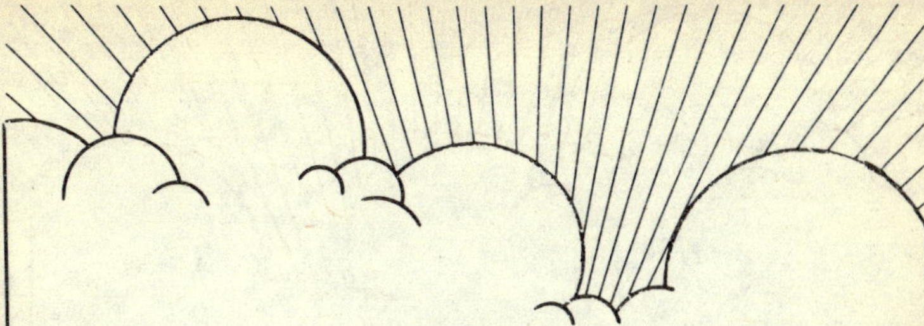

Welcome to HEAVEN

THE ARRIVAL

They say that the way to arrive at Istanbul or Venice is to sail in at dawn. They say too that when the aircraft door is thrown open after you've landed at Calcutta airport, the smell that greets you is never forgotten. Every new land is rich in first impressions and, as you stumble from the top of the escalator onto the world above, Heaven, shining before you, is no exception. You've arrived at the gates of the new Jerusalem. What do you see and what should you do?

The first thing to catch your eye will undoubtedly be the walls. Though not yet the promised walls of the Book of Revelation, they are still a magnificient spectacle in the rich and hallowed golden light. Those who now look far to the left will see the point on the walls from where Lucifer and his followers made their timely exit. Be warned. Ancient as this spot may be, it survives to serve a future purpose should the need arise. Below this spot is Noah's tavern, where Noah is happy to serve anyone waiting for their admissions interview. Take Dutch courage by all means, but don't spoil your chances or you might end up in the drink as Noah did himself (as he'll certainly tell you given half a chance!).

The admission procedure itself usually lasts twenty-four hours and you'll be offered accommodation this time in one of the overnight hospices located in the walls themselves (Noah's closes at 11.00 pm each night, 10.30 pm on Sundays by order). During this time you'll be asked to give a full account of your previous life and to explain your reasons for wanting Heavenly citizenship. Rest assured, there are no formal requirements, no visas, work permits, National Insurance contributions, CSEs or work experience. Rather, there is an unwritten law that everyone must be given a fair hearing and a firm agreement that once admitted, you're in for life (or for life hereafter!).

The history of the Pearly Gates can be found elsewhere (page 98). Here we have concentrated on providing useful hints for new arrivals. Do *always* tell the truth. There is absolutely no point in trying to lie about the past. Remember that the authorities already know more about you than you know yourself. They have a minute-by-minute computer profile of your life from birth to death. This details every possible aspect of everything that you've ever done, or considered doing. As if that wasn't formidable enough, the authorities will also have cross-checked it with other people's records and accounts of the same incidents to provide an infallible guide to your character.

In fact the only reason why St Peter's team bother to ask you questions at all is to enable you to give your side of the story. They know the facts. They want to see what you make of them. So, play it straight, say your piece and hope that they've seen it that way too. If it's any consolation they're not trying to catch you out. Just stay calm and relaxed when you're called in. (You might try helping yourself by getting a bit of repenting done now before it's too late.)

A note about Customs declarations
Bearing in mind that the authorities know in advance exactly what you're hiding away in your brain, it is essential that you always go through the red channel marked **Confessions/Something to Declare**. Then is the time to admit to reading Karl Marx in the lavatory at school, or Frank Harris, while your folks were out. Experience has shown time and again that it's far better to pay up and clear your mind at this stage than literally to be hauled over the coals later on. So, if there's any dialectical materialism tucked away in your cerebral luggage, or even a few grams of atheism secreted up one nostril, get rid of them now.

WHERE TO STAY

In keeping with the relaxed egalitarianism that's a way of life in the hereafter, accommodation in Heaven is mercifully free from the cut-throat hotel operators that have bedevilled so many of the time-honoured destinations most of us are used to. For one thing, in Heaven there is no official classification of hotels and other accommodation. For another there are no fixed prices, for the simple reason that there are no prices. Smiling benignly on newcomers and long-stay visitors alike, the authorities provide subsidised accommodation for all. But that doesn't mean that there isn't any choice. The sky's the limit when you're in Heaven and that goes for accommodation as it does for everything else.

As part of its long-term, forward-thinking development programme the Divine Planning Authority (or DPA) has cast its net far and wide to embrace architectural styles to suit every individual taste. Visitors can choose to stay in the cosy intimacy of a self-catering cave or may prefer a grotto offering a taste of the true anchorite life for the robust and hardy. Many visitors, of course, are after greater ease and magnificence and go for the opulent splendour of a cardinal's palace, or a replica of the Osmond home. The choice is yours, and you, like millions of others, may look on your time in Heaven as a complete break with what has gone before and so choose the style of accommodation that best allows you to feel that you have got away from it all.

It has to be admitted that while the facilities in the most up-to-date hotels in the metropolis excel any you'll ever have encountered, those in the remoter regions have a rustic charm and simplicity that is not to everyone's taste. Nevertheless, there is much to be said for the determined in spirit who take off into the Wilderness on the special forty-day retreat. Stockbrokers, life insurance salesmen, bookmakers and systems analysts are often to be found having the time of their lives grubbing around in search of hopeful looking stones and other less obvious forms of sustenance. Similarly the sometime inhabitants of the earth's more grandiose and flamboyant homes often choose to settle down to an idyllic existence in a Heavenly semi on the outskirts of the main centres.

So given a wide choice, what is really on offer when you arrive?

Your First Night

As there's no certainty that you'll be admitted to Heaven, it follows that there is no possibility of booking your accommodation in advance. It also follows that there's no refund if your stay is cancelled indefinitely.

For the chosen ones who pass through the Pearly Gates the YHA (Young Heavonians Association) has laid on a well-advertised scheme to help you settle in. Make their information office (first building on the right after St Marks and St Spencer) your first port of call. Behind the reception desk you'll always be sure to find a cherubic smile and a friendly 'Peace be with you'. The staff are some of the most experienced in Heaven. Many of them have spent what seems like eternity familiarising themselves with the different types of visitor that pass through their office every year. Gabriel, now one of the senior management committee, still makes occasional trips into the field to keep abreast of the latest developments. If you're lucky, you may catch a glimpse of him from the outer office, either working busily at his desk or preparing to dash off with another batch of tidings. But even if the faces are unfamiliar to you they'll always be welcoming.

The job of the YHA is to find each visitor a room straightaway. If there isn't a room available then they'll arrange for someone to build you one there and then. This only takes a few hours, during which you can taste your first of many milk and honey cocktails and maybe sample a little local manna in one of the delightful cafés that you'll discover in Heaven proper. Our advice would be to go easy on the manna at first. It's an acquired taste, like red chillies and retsina. After all, you've plenty of time to get to know its subtleties and to learn to relish its gastronomic delights. Anyway your YHA room will certainly be completed before dusk. Construction work always finished before dark in Heaven.

As with all other heavenly accommodation your room can be tailored to your particular requirements. Interior flying buttresses, lofty, vaulted ceilings, severe romanesque chancels, you name them, you can have them. Most visitors, especially the humble and meek, usually go for something grand on their first night. Cathedrals are very popular, if a little draughty. But after the almost agoraphobic vastness of the journey, massive rooms like these can be a gentle way of getting used to a more confined existence once again.

Decor too is left to the individual visitor. Giotto has been working round the clock in recent years painting frescoes for newcomers, and at time of going to print has closed his order books for the next millennium. Rubens, though, has fallen from favour recently and his services can be hired for a very competitive sum. For those who like their surroundings plain, the Reformation Interior Design and Decorating Co. can come up with a YHA room as white as the purest soul. So while you're idling away your time on the way up, why not do a little wishful thinking and picture where and how you'd like to spend your first night inside the Pearly Gates.

Hotels

Although there is no limit to your stay in a YHA room, most visitors yearn for a taste of the real Heaven soon after their arrival. This is perfectly understandable and the YHA staff are always on hand to help you choose where to move next. (Kind as they always are and, at times, helpful almost to a fault, you should not offer to tip them under any circumstances. It may be better to give than to receive on Earth. But up there, let them do the giving at first. Your own time will come.)

Only one word can describe Heaven's hotels – Lordly. In every way they breathe confident magnificence and exude gentle omnipotence. The hotels themselves are so different that each one is a discovery in itself and who are we to rob you of that discovery? But one or two general details may be of help and these we willingly include.

Every hotel has rooms with en suite chapels. You'll find that room service offers a resident prophet to help you plan ahead. Outdoor activities are well catered for, though don't ask for hunting, shooting, or fishing licences. Remember where you are! Ladies are no longer required to wear hats all the time, nor should they necessarily keep their arms covered, but as you'll quickly get used to the vestments provided there's little worry that you'll cause offence in any of the Lord's houses. Swimming and table tennis have grown immensely in popularity in Heaven in recent years, but again remember that there is no sense of competition in any of these activities. The first shall be last and the last shall be first. Those who have made it are all winners. Count yourself lucky and leave it at that.

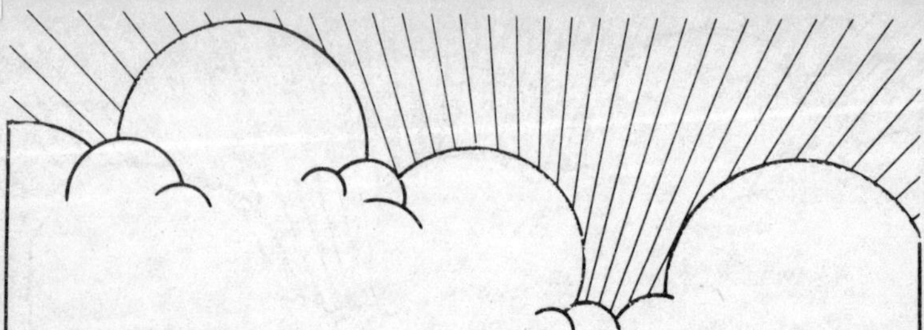

Other Accommodation

Like all the best centres Heaven has a variety of places to stay. If the formality of the large hotels is not to your liking then you'll certainly be on the look-out for either a Guest House/Boarding House, or a Self-Catering Heavenly Apartment.

Most Guest Houses/Boarding Houses have homely cuisine and the intimacy that has become associated with Heavenly families. Don't look for all mod cons and don't be surprised to find yourself in what looks suspiciously like a stable. These simple down-to-earth homes will give you a taste of Heaven as it used to be.

With Self-Catering Heavenly Apartments you can go one step further and fend for yourself. These offer the greatest privacy to the visitor. If you want to stay in bed all day, if you want to walk around in sackcloth and ashes, if you want to fast for weeks on end, that's your business. No one will be criticising or attempt to interfere. Bear in mind, however, that as there's no charge for accommodation in Heaven, you don't save anything by going for a self-catering cell. The choice is entirely yours.

In addition to the accommodation mentioned above visitors shouldn't overlook the facilities that exist in other areas away from Greater Heaven. Portachurches, Sanctuariums, Bed & Fasts, Penitence Inns and Caraclouds are all available. Again, ask at the YHA office for full details.

Take your pick, we're sure that you'll have a glorious time.

A Home of Your Own

Such are the delights of Heaven that it's not surprising that nearly all visitors decide to settle permanently and sooner or later start looking around for a home of their own.

The agency that handles all property transactions in Heaven is the Agent of Holy Estate. There are branches in all the main centres where you can get first-hand, personal advice as well as reviewing what is on the market. It's only fair to warn prospective buyers, especially those who have been through the process of acquiring a house or flat on Earth, that they'll be in for a shock when they call at their local office. The blatant honesty and integrity of the local staff takes some getting used to. You'll find that Heavenly estate agents will spend most of their time trying to help you! Some may even try to persuade you to go to another office if their own stock doesn't meet your requirements. You'll find too that there is a predominant local habit of insisting that the agent pays for all house surveys out of his or her own money bag. Don't try to resist this. It is part of a heritage that stretches back further than time itself. This spirit is inbred and nothing that you or the Earth below can do will change the situation.

The agent will also assist you in arranging a mortgage, should you need one. Be careful though that your agent doesn't try to pay your mortgage for you. This is an alarming tendency that has been increasingly reported in recent years. If such an offer is made, you should refuse it in no uncertain terms. Let this slip past unnoticed, or turn a blind eye to it, and you'll find your agent paying all your other bills and in very extreme cases paying huge cheques into your account as well. Not only is this a bit tiresome, but quite frankly there's no reason why anyone should find it difficult to meet their repayments at all. The reason for this is perfectly simple. As you're in Heaven for life, which for all practical purposes means infinity, the repayment period for any loan (including mortgages) can be literally for ever. The implication is that any loan repayments can be so thinned down by extending the repayment periods as to reduce the repayment sum to a pittance. Just as the customary period for an Earth mortgage is twenty-five years, a mortgage in Heaven is something of the order of twenty-five million years. Therefore, if you speak to a mortgage broker in Heaven (and there is only one since two would breed competition – a nasty little vice that is strongly discouraged) he will be able to arrange a mortgage for any amount of money over any amount of time. If it sounds miraculous, that's because it is.

Assuming then that you do decide to buy a house, what should you look for? You know that you're going to get an honest deal from your agent. You know too that you can afford any property you like. What's more, you also have the insurance that where on Earth 'an act of God' usually spells disaster to the house owner, in Heaven it's the exact reverse. Should anything go wrong, or should any vital work need doing on your future home, there's always an angel of the Lord on hand to perform a fully proficient miracle. These include silicone injection damp-proof coursing in thirty seconds, re-roofing in twenty minutes (thirty minutes if there's a Heavenly shower) and a full loft conversion to Heavenly building regulations in a minute and a half. So, what's to stop you going out and buying the biggest house available? In a nutshell there are two things.

First, all houses in Heaven are exactly the same: each has ninety-six bedrooms, thirty-four reception rooms, a fully-fitted cathedral, which conveniently doubles as an entrance hall, off which leads the self-contained, doorless sauna (another of the Heavenly creations). This means there's plenty of room to accommodate friends or members of the family who may be joining you in the hereafter.

The second reason for not rushing out to buy the most expensive house you can lay your hand on is that you won't feel the compelling greed any longer. Once you enter the Pearly Gates, your avarice is purged from you. Your former craving for the biggest and the best of everything is replaced by a meek satisfaction with the smallest and

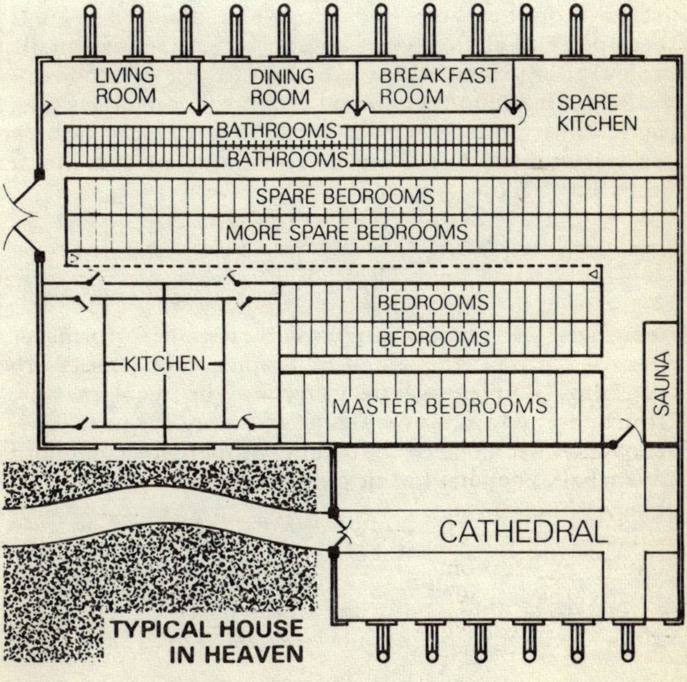

TYPICAL HOUSE IN HEAVEN

humblest – in relative terms. In the same way houses near the centre of Heaven are no more or less popular than houses on the outskirts. In Heaven the laws of economics and finance simply don't apply. That some people get a house near the centre of Heaven sooner than others is of no concern. As time is infinite, everyone's turn comes eventually and with time on one's side the difference between a month or a millennium has no bearing at all.

It all sounds a very satisfying experience and it would be, if such mortal pleasures held any value in Paradise – but they don't. Finding yourself a nice house is totally irrelevant to people in Heaven. One of the great ironies of this trip of a lifetime is that on Earth most of us strive for a bigger house and occasionally get it, while in Heaven there is no striving and we are given it without question. It's a funny life, isn't it?

ETIQUETTE

Heaven is refreshingly simple with regard to forms of address. Only in Russia and in Trappist monasteries are the forms simpler. Nearly everyone you meet may be referred to by their name; Christian names if you are well acquainted, surnames if the meeting is more formal. There are three exceptions to this general rule:

The Lord There are a number of correct forms of address given in the Bible. 'Father Almighty', 'Lord', 'Heavenly Father' are good standbys. Don't make your greetings too flowery. Keep them short and to the point.

Saints Generally these should be referred to as Saint Luke etc., except when you are addressing the saint directly in which case the form 'Saint' is used.

Angels It is customary not to speak directly to angels. (See the section on angels.)

In all other cases it is perfectly in order for you to open a conversation. The Lord blessed you with the gift of speech, so go ahead and show him what you can do with it. By the same token you should be prepared to listen as well. As you were provided with two ears, but only one mouth, you should try to conduct your conversations so that you only speak a third of the time and listen for two-thirds of the time. Genetic engineering was no fluke. The Lord had quite definite plans when he designed the human body, and you should pay due regard to what he laid down in the physical form. More often than not you'll find the answer on how you should behave by taking a quick peep at your own body.

Many visitors find it useful to familiarise themselves with other forms of communication as well as the more obvious ones. Sign, body and eye languages all have a part to play in Heavenly conduct and the language of throwing rosary water can have a profound influence on the right audience. It is a little known fact that when the Pope throws water over the masses in St Peter's Square on Earth he is also carrying out an elaborate coded conversation with the Lord above.

The language of Heaven itself is discussed elsewhere, but there are one or two pointers on general etiquette that the reader would find of use when arriving in Heaven. For an essentially informal society, Heaven does lay down certain curiously formal customs and habits, with which the visitor is expected to accord. Obviously the finer details and nuances can be picked up while you are there, but in essence the rules are:

1. Never pray with your mouth full.
2. Don't wear brown sandals with a blue halo.
3. Don't carry your wings slung over one shoulder or in your pockets. (This applies to Angels only.)
4. Don't whistle through your teeth.
5. Always keep a box of tissues hidden in your raiments or vestments (for emergencies).
6. If going into the Wilderness for any length of time, don't forget to take a razor and a toothbrush. These should be labelled carefully to avoid any unpleasant confusion when you finally come to use them.
7. If going away for any length of time be sure to pack a spare halo.
8. Don't walk across any water if you've got a verruca.
9. If you wear sandals be sure not to wear socks underneath.
10. Whenever crossing a road always use the Holy Cross Code.
11. The traditional toast when drinking casually is 'The blood of Christ' not 'Bottoms up'.
12. It is no longer acceptable to present your host with a bottle of water hoping that he will turn it into wine. Nor should you present him with a rock and hope for water to come forth.

EATING

Heavenly food shares many characteristics with food on Earth. Indeed the visitor will be delighted at the range and universal excellence of everything that is offered by the generous and hospitable inhabitants of this land of plenty. Local specialities rub shoulders with familiar dishes from home, but alas, to little avail, because you'll find that after entering Heaven your appetite tends to wane. This is nothing serious and is certainly no cause for alarm. It doesn't indicate that you're sickening for anything. It's more a case of nourishment of the body finally taking a very definite second place to nourishment of the soul in the land of Our Father. So, in spite of mouthwatering dishes groaning with every delicacy you could ever wish for, your mouth will remain distinctly unwatered.

In fact, you'll find that many of the old Heaven-hands prefer to while away the evening over a bowl of cold porridge and a lump of mouldy bread. They find a special virtue in eschewing the best of Heavenly haute cuisine and surprisingly the only time when the residents of Heaven really indulge themselves in a slap-up meal is when they're under the weather. They maintain that this is a wonderful tonic for the spirit and a challenge to their resolve. Visitors are advised to follow their example with extreme caution at first.

In general no matter what your taste in food may be, you can be certain that somewhere in Heaven you'll find exactly what you're looking for, even though it won't be in the least bit appetising when you do finally track it down.

If you're the sort who likes to search out the local specialities then in Heaven you'll want to keep your eyes open for places advertising fast foods. These are simple, convenient meals that have become very popular in Heaven over the years and to many people have come to symbolise Heavenly catering. Fast foods are specially prepared, prepacked meals of nothing, as their name implies. They are the original meals-for-none. Fast foods take many forms, but the most commonly served consist of trays of delicious three or five-course meals which you collect from one counter and carry to a table. There a waitress takes the loaded tray from you and carries it back to the kitchen where it can be served up to the next customer. All is ease and simplicity and you don't run the risk of spilling soup or custard down your dazzling white vestments.

Drinking in Heaven is an acquired taste. We mentioned Noah's tavern earlier, but this is outside the walls. Inside Heaven things are different. Heaven is essentially teetotal. Milk and honey cocktails are sold in abundance, but like the Coca Colas which sell by the million in the Muslim world, they seldom satisfy the hardened drinker from Earth. Sad to say, there's nothing in Heaven that does. Popular demand has forced the opening of several English-style pubs in the metropolis. These have the authentic stamp of English pubs on Earth, complete with their licensing hours – the only differences being that they are friendly and don't try to pass their water off as beer. If you think you might enjoy a pure pint at the pub, we recommend the 'Pig and Missionary', the 'Elephant and Presbyterian', the 'Methodist's Arms' and the 'Cardinal's Error'.

Heavenly pubs are ideal places too to study the residents in their free time. Relaxed, jovial and heartwarming these friendly homes from home are used to welcoming strangers to their midst. Don't hold back. Push your way through the cheerful celestial throng at the bar – you're all equal in the eyes of the Lord anyhow – and order a pint of foaming, nut-brown void. Raise this to your lips and set your imagination whirring. Your mind will take care of the rest and you won't have a ghastly hangover the following morning. If it tastes like nothing on earth, it'll be even more familiar.

As a coda we ought to point out that if you're the sort in search of a cup of tea just like mother used to make it ... then so are we!

ENTERTAINMENT

While it's true to say that the bulk of your time in Heaven will be taken up with praying, praying and more praying, there will be times when you feel like relaxing and consequently not enjoying yourself. At times like this your thoughts may veer to one of the many entertainments and pastimes that Heaven has laid on for the visitor and resident alike.

Sport We must preface our remarks with the observation that most sports in Heaven are communal and that individual sports are not encouraged on the grounds that they develop too great a sense of personal fulfilment and independence. In short they are myopic and selfish.

Team games are not without their own problems either. Experiments with eleven-a-side table tennis led to disastrous congestion and several crumpled wings and dented haloes. But these were minor problems in the face of the major crisis that confronts sport in Heaven today – sportsmanship. The egalitarianism and good nature that have made Heaven the acme of attainment in so many spheres have wrought havoc in competition. In Heaven, where consideration and fair play are bywords adhered to by all, chaos is swift to ensue. A typical example of this is the game of cricket.

So keen are cricket sides to see that the rules are observed and the spirit of the game respected that many batsmen walk from the crease even before they have faced a ball because they consider that the bowler is good enough to bowl them out and therefore *deserves* to bowl them out. There have been equally confusing confrontations in which batsmen have appealed for their own dismissal while the fielding side have insisted that they remain at the wicket.

This confusion is not restricted to cricket, alas. In the case of many ball games both sides have felt it better to do away with the ball altogether. They prefer to come to a mutual agreement on the course of the game and its eventual result while they are still in the dressing room. This is a situation that none of the players object to in the slightest, but it does leave some spectators both perplexed and disappointed.

Other sports have suffered too from the modifications necessary to make them acceptable in the Heavenly Kingdom. Boxing, for example, long ago banned the hitting of one opponent by the other. As a result players now shadow box without laying a punch on each other until one boxer collapses through exhaustion or sheer boredom. The same goes for wrestling in which physical contact between wrestlers is banned altogether. To avoid any risk of this rule being transgressed, wrestlers now enter the ring independently and wrestle with themselves. As the winner is still decided in the traditional way with three falls, three submissions or a knockout, and no one has ever fallen, submitted or been knocked out (except for one competitor who slipped while climbing into the ring) the result is invariably a draw.

A further adaptation of the rules brought about a popular local variant of the sport: Theological Wrestling. In this groups gather together to wrestle with knotty ecclesiastical or moral issues. The excitement engendered by topics like 'Was Paul right?' is only partially marred by the scoring system which is again limited to three falls, three submissions or a knockout. Since these never occur, there are never any winners.

To sum up, every sport in Heaven has undergone changes, and our advice is to go along and join in, but be prepared neither to win nor to lose and not to mind one way or the other.

Theatre/Cinema/Music Unfortunately it has to be admitted that the overbearing piousness of the kingdom has left its mark on the stage and the screen. This is no product of the censor's pen. Those wishing to see blue movies, for example, no doubt could. There don't happen to be any people like that in Heaven, that's all. Over the millennia a sort of tacit understanding between performers and their audiences has resulted in a very narrow band of entertainment. This usually takes the form of a folk concert underpinned by evangelism in which words, music and prayers form the principal components. It may come as a surprise that William Shakespeare, a resident of Heaven for some five hundred years in spite of the episode with the poached game and one or two *risqué* lines, can still only get his plays staged by low-budget repertory companies, and this is in spite of writing better plays than ever.

The cinema does little to broaden this narrow artistic path. Films are merely screen versions of what is being staged in theatres all over Heaven. And the same is true of Heavenly music, with its monotonous, if blessedly dulcet obsession with the harp. (The music of the spheres, so popular in former times, has more or less disappeared from the popular current repertoire. Such is progress.)

Of course, if you are hell-bent on seeing a good film or a re-run of *Dallas* you might question whether Heaven is really the place for you. After all, there is another place in the afterlife that is dedicated to the provisions of continuous entertainment, and for which an earthly life glued to the television is admirable training.

In spite of their lack of suitable qualifications, many performing artists do find their way inside the Pearly Gates, perhaps as a reward for playing working men's clubs or the Citizens' Theatre, Glasgow, year in year out. Even so their Heavenly activities are usually restricted to the fringes. But then we shouldn't lose sight of where we are. This may be Paradise, but it's also a holy land – and there's nothing particularly holy about being entertained.

Heavenly television is still in its infancy. Two channels broadcast a selection of religious and biblical programmes for a total of three hours every day. The remaining air-time is taken up with educational programmes and with re-runs of *Ben-Hur*, *The Ten Commandments*, *The Sound of Music*, *Carry on Converting* and *Quo Vadis*, to mention just a few of the officially sanctioned imports from the world below.

Pastimes Pastimes are little talked about and little indulged in. Embroidery (for altar cloths and prayer mats) is occasionally undertaken. Carpentry is widespread and it is noticeable that most of God's children can still turn out a beautifully worked piece of wood when they put their mind to it. Other than these, handicrafts and DIY have still to catch on in Heaven. Historical isolation has impeded the spread of space invaders and bingo, and rigorous customs checks have forestalled the entry of other undesirable pursuits and practices. But Heaven is a broad-minded land for all that and should you wish to pursue a harmless hobby on the other side of the stars you'll find that every facility will be made available to help you. If woodwork and handicrafts are your particular interests, you'll be pleased to know that you don't need to take your own tools since all the equipment you need will be provided. Another bonus is that you will suddenly discover that on passing through the Pearly Gates you'll become ambidextrous, which will make life a great deal easier.

SPECIAL EVENTS

There are certain annual events, festivals and holidays that you won't want to miss, so be sure to make a note of them in your diary.

Jan 1	Herods Sale
Jan 18–Feb 16	Plague of Locusts Exhibition
Feb 28	Display of Massed Sinning by the combined bands of Sodom and Gomorrah

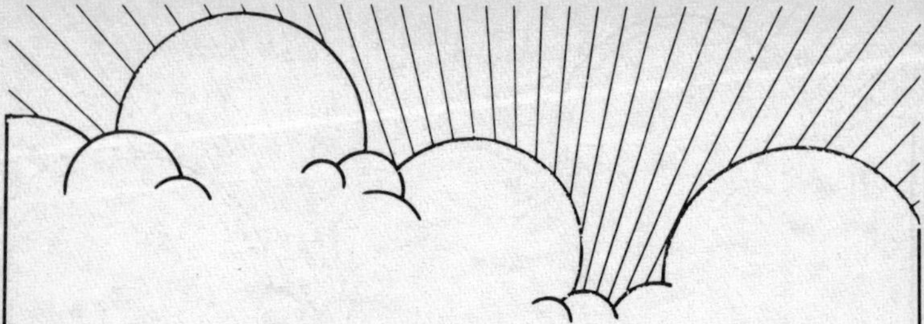

Feb 29	Display of Massed Forgiveness by the bands of the Heavenly Choir in Vestibule
March 21	CUP FINAL: Gladiator's United v. Ash Wednesday
April 14	Temptation Season begins
April 29	FINAL of *It's a Flock Out* (more madcapped fun and games with the Lord's Shepherd)
May 1	Day of Judgement (Bank Holiday)
June 22	Final round of Moto-Cross (religious motor sport)
August 3	Miss Heaven Finals
Sept 14	Formation praying (from the Kingdom of Heaven Slipper Baths)
Sept 23	Pro-Am reincarnation
Oct 11	*Genesis Live!* (rare appearance of this now legendary Biblical phenomena)
Nov 23–25	International Healing from Lourdes
Nov 29–30	Custom Shroud Show
Dec 5	Hell Drivers World Championship (live from Hell)

EXCURSIONS

Visiting the Earth as a Ghost

In spite of Heaven's undeniable attractions, there is a time in everyone's stay there when the call from below becomes irresistible. The desire to look up old friends and visit familiar places is a natural spiritual response and the authorities, acknowledging this, have established The

Reunion Club, which has the job of sending departed souls back to Earth as ghosts.

One of the paradoxes about this otherwise worthy organisation is that it has doggedly refused to move with the times. Whereas so much of the best of modern technology has been imported into Heaven for the well-being of its residents and visitors, little or nothing has been done to improve the lot of the ghost. As is often the case with nebulous issues such as theirs, ghosts have been frankly neglected. Only a small amount of expenditure could help change their image and identity beyond measure. Instead of appearing as indistinct, shadowy figures that scare the living daylights out of those they have gone to visit, a little simple modernisation could render bold, full-colour ghosts with either matt or gloss finishes. In the same way the handicap that has bedevilled ghosts for so long, their inability to communicate, could easily be rectified with the incorporation of speech mechanisms (though there are some who would quibble about the word 'incorporation').

The truth of the matter is that ghosts don't have much standing in Heaven. The powers that be have long since failed to smile upon them and while ghosts have not been banned outright, it is painfully apparent that little effort or money is spent in approving their appearance, life-style and image.

That said, it must be admitted that The Reunion Club does its best in paving the way for your earthly visitations. They have a full range of costumes that are available to all for very modest rates (these are waived in the case of ex-Equity members). But their most important role is one of instruction. The Reunion Club spends most of its limited funds in the very sensitive task of spiritual counselling.

The Club's instructors are concerned above all else to minimise the shock caused to loved ones and others on Earth when the departed reappears. They teach would-be ghosts how to avoid creaking staircases and noisy doors. They give lessons in ways of avoiding detection and in covering your tracks. There's even a course on how to explain things in the unlikely event of your being caught – not an easy thing to do when you can't speak. (For those wishing to return to Earth as something other than a straightforward ghost it's only fair to point out that there is a long waiting list. The Lord himself has soul responsibility for choosing successful candidates: after all we can't have Earth overrun with headless horsemen.

One question that is frequently asked on the subject of ghosts is, 'Do Earthly seances reach the ears of those who are called?' The answer is sadly a very definite 'No'. It would be impossible to try to respond to all such requests, especially in the case of famous souls who receive upwards of a hundred calls every day. It would also be very unfair to make souls constantly pop down to Earth simply because Auntie wants to know the winner of the 4.15 at Redcar. The number of times that a dear departed is summoned and seems to appear must just be put down to coincidence. Because there are a remarkable number of ghosts floating about it's quite likely that, given the numbers, a few sightings do coincide with seances on Earth.

If a dear departed soul wants to visit a relative or friend on Earth, he or she will. No amount of pressure or coercion from below will have any effect on their resolve one way or the other.

A Day Trip to Hell

Though not far away in distance, Hell and Heaven are poles apart in terms of spiritual contact. Visiting Hell is actively discouraged and the authorities make no effort to disguise the fact that those wishing to visit Hell are made to face many official obstacles. However, there are two factors that prevent a total ban on trips to Hell.

In the first place Heaven is a democracy, or at least as much of a democracy as anywhere ruled over by one being can be. For this reason the press and television are free from censorship and looking through the small ads in the back of many newspapers you'll find advertisements that encourage you to visit 'the other place'. As you might expect, these are unequivocal in their message. They're brash, they're bright and they don't miss a trick in trying to win you over to the idea. The one positive advantage they do have is that they provide all the details about visiting Hell that the authorities in Heaven takes steps to confuse and suppress.

Secondly a complete ban on visiting Hell would go against the essential principle on which Heaven was founded. It would be too dogmatic and unbending. So, if your heart is really set on going to have a look at Hell you will be allowed out, providing you can cope with the mass of red tape that will confront you before permission is granted. 'Getting permission to go to Hell is like a Russian trying to get a week-end break in Las Vegas.' (In his case the Russian met with greater success!)

The mass of paperwork that you'll have to fill in is truly mind boggling. Every statement must be accompanied by a written declaration, countersigned by fifty souls. Every aspect of your trip will be scrutinised; your intentions, your itinerary, your accommodation, nothing will be left unexamined. You'll have to account for every second you spend in Hell *in advance*. Above all you'll have to present concrete evidence that your visit to Hell has nothing whatsoever to do with sin. This generally entails an application for 'missionary status', by which you unofficially swear that your sole purpose in visiting Hell is to spread 'the word'.

Once you've got through the paperwork you'll be required to undergo a full medical examination. This takes note of every mark and scratch on your body, the details of which are assiduously recorded. On your return you'll be asked to undergo an identical examination and Heaven help anyone who's marks don't match. One illicit love bite and you'll be up before the Almighty faster than you can say 'Redeem Me'.

It's not surprising that many aspiring visitors to Hell find their enthusiasm crushed by the weight of this bureaucracy. All we can say in its defence is 'Quite right too!' You're not supposed to be going to Hell in search of a good time. In theory, at least, you're supposed to be on a mission of mercy, to spread the word to miserable sinners.

Curiously, when you get to Hell you won't find many colourful villains. In fact you may be surprised by how peaceful and calm the whole place seems to be. You'll see people going about their daily torment without appearing to sin openly. You may even detect a general air of contentment which can come as something of a shock to the uninitiated.

It can't be emphasised too strongly that the Hell we read about in the Bible tends to be somewhat overplayed. There is a fiery furnace and there are pits of eternal damnation into which people accidentally fall from time to time. But the image of the land dripping with blood is best left to the testaments.

That said, it must be stressed that Hell isn't a particularly attractive place to live. It's a giant, sprawling conurbation with an unpleasantly humid climate and an annoying throbbing sound that causes continual headaches to all who live there. It stinks as well. The smell of Hell is a sickening odour, a cross between boiled eggs and a very sweet flower. The stench hangs in one's nostrils and permeates one's clothes and hair. It gets everywhere else too. There are hundreds of different air-fresheners on the market that aim to combat the awful aroma, but the most they manage to do is replace one repulsive smell with another. Hell's other major sensation is boredom, a relentless gnawing boredom that drains even the most resolute souls of enthusiasm and activity.

Of course you will find sin in Hell if you really want it. It's not the glamorous skin-tingling sin that is normally associated with Hell, not the seething mass of orgiastic debauchery that many secretly yearn for. Sin in Hell amounts to a sordid series of pathetic inadequacies heavily tinged with tedium. Disappointing as this may sound, it has one positive advantage for the visitor. Even if you were foolishly tempted to go back on your word and have a taste of sin, you'd find it hard to find anything worthwhile to do.

There is no doubt that visitors to Hell don't enjoy it in the same way as the residents. Full details of how to get there on a permanent basis will be given in our companion volume, *Go to Hell!* (not yet published). To give a flavour of what's involved, here is a sample of the preliminary application form that all the determinedly Hell-bent have to complete.

APPLICATION FORM FOR HELL

Name ....

Age ....

Address ....

1. Previous Sins (approximate number) ....
2. Favourite Sin ....
3. Is there any sin you don't like ....
4. What's your favourite colour ....
   a) if blood (specify whose blood) ....
   b) if not blood say why (and it had better be good) ....
5. Do you smell ☐ Yes ☐ No
   if yes say where ....
6. Have you ever been convicted of a criminal offence
   ☐ Yes ☐ No
   if not why not ....
7. Can you spell criminal offence ☐ Yes ☐ No
8. Which of these descriptions best fits you
   ☐ RUDE & VIOLENT
   ☐ RUDE & VIOLENT
   ☐ CRUDE & VIOLENT
   ☐ CRUDE & VIOLENT & AGGRESSIVE
9. Please arrange the following vices in the order you would commit them (if all at the same time write 'together'): Illicit sex/boosing/swearing/kicking people/nicking stuff/ wrecking public property/lying/blowing nose without a

handkerchief/smoking in a non-smoker/drugs/GBH/vandalism
1.
2.
3.
4.
5.
6.
7.
8.
9.
10.
11.
12.

10. Now add three more categories of your own ....
11. Please add a piece of graffiti ....
12. If given a place in Hell how would you try and ruin it for everyone else ....
13. How many pints do you drink a day   To the nearest ten.
14. What are these pints of ....
15. Are you a pervert ☐ Yes ☐ Yes ☐ Yes
16. Do you clean your teeth at all
    ☐ No ☐ Yes (with a power drill) ☐ What teeth
17. Are you prepared to grow two little horns
    ☐Yes ☐ Where
18. Are you prepared to grow a short black beard
    ☐ Yes ☐ Yes
    (Women)

Signed: .... Dated: ....

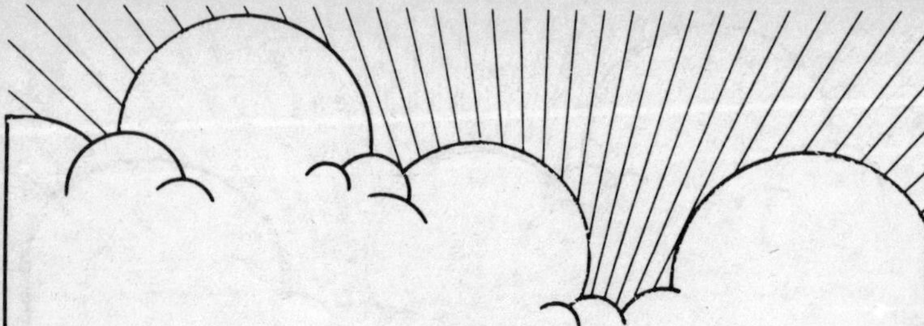

The White Pages

HEAVEN – THE FACTS AT A GLANCE

Official Name	The United Kingdom of Heaven
Capital	Heaven
Other Major Cities	Heaven, Heaven, Heaven, Heaven, Heaven, Heaven, Heaven, Heaven, Heaven, Heaven, Heaven, Heaven, Heaven-on-Earth
Major Rivers	Heaven, Heaven, Heaven, Heaven, Heaven, Rio Heaven, Heaven, Styx
Major Mountain Range	The Celestial Heights
Climate	Benign. Some cloud formations at lower levels
Currency	Goodwill. 1 Goodwill = 100 Kind Thoughts Rate of Exchange = at par with earthly currencies

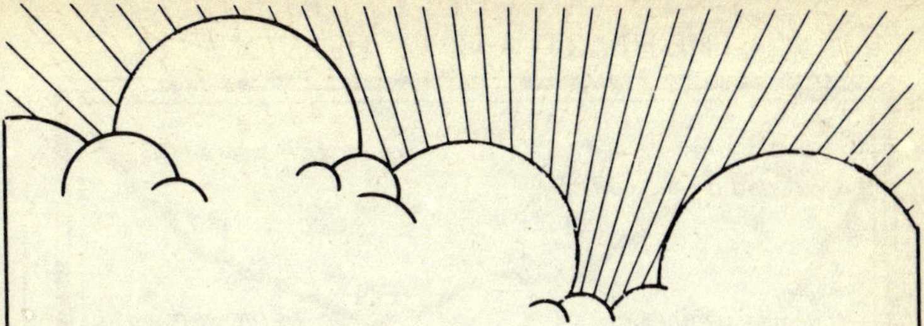

Area	Infinite
Population	If you're lucky
Principal Exports	Love, peace, understanding, wrath
Language	Tongues
Measurements	Cubits, talents, scores
Telephones	No
Foreign Language Newspapers	*The Christian Science Monitor,* Parish magazines (any number thereof). All other publications are available in translation (also any number thereof)
Death Rate	Nil
Taxation Rate	0 per cent
National Flag	White cross set on a white and white striped background with a white border.
Early Closing Day	Judgement Day

THE HEARTLAND OF HEAVEN

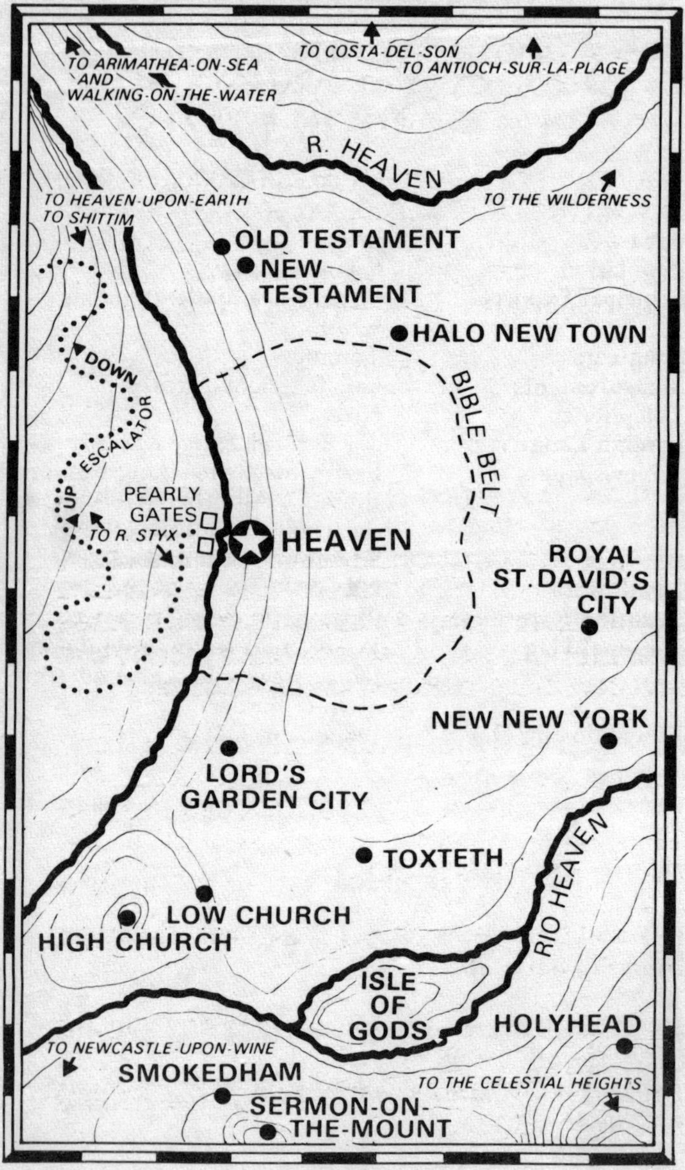

LORD'S GARDEN CITY Pop 3,000,000,000,000,000,000,000,000 3,000,000,000 Mon, Tue, Fri. **Lord's Arms** **El Vino's**

HEAVEN-UPON-EARTH Pop 2,000,000,000,000,000,000,000,000,000,000,000,000,000,000,000,000,000 (continued on page 144) 2,000,000,000,000,000 Mon, Tue, Wed, Thur, Fri
Travailodge Motel LC LP

NEWCASTLE-UPON-WINE Pop 5,000,000,000,000,000,000,000,000,000,001 2 MD Sabbath
The Geasey Prayer Book

SHITTIM a [redacted] place on the [redacted] mountains north of Moab across the [redacted] Jordan [redacted] from Jericho [redacted]

HALO NEW TOWN Pop 6,000,000,000,000,000,000,000,000,000,000,000 243,387,476,290,198,362,093,987,039,987,038,098,098,098, (continued on page 144) MD Tuesday
The Pig & Whistle

THE WILDERNESS Pop 1 Mon, Tue, Wed, Thur, Fri, Sat, Sab.

ARIMATHEA-ON-SEA Pop 243,987,398,465 847 496 26
The St. Julie Andrews 96 FULHAM 10 LIVERPOOL 0
9.30 300

ROYAL-ST. DAVID'S CITY Pop 9,000,000, 000,000,000,000,000,000,001 9,000,000, 000,000,000,000,000,000,001 MD Mon Wed Mon, Fri **The Heaven Astoria** ††††††††††† LATE **The Railway Arms** 1 1 FULHAM 0 LIVERPOOL 0 **The Railway Legs** (closed for demolition)

WALKING-ON-THE-WATER Pop 3,000,000,000, 000,000,000,000,000,000,000 (this population is only approximate it is believed to be true to the best of our knowledge — the mayor) Wed MD Tue
Sealink-Arms 96
Walking On The Water Hydro CD

ISLE OF GODS Pop 3½ Wed Sabbath

SMOKEDHAM Pop N.A. N.A. N.A. N.A.

ANTIOCH-SUR-LA-PLAGE Pop 3,263,762,983, 109,276,190,271, 485,907 Thur
The Grand LP LC CD ALC

The Very Grand ††††† 116
The Very Very Grand †††††††††††††††††††
(continued on page 104)

TOXTETH Pop 0

EXPLANATIONS OF SYMBOLS USED

†	*RECOMMENDED BUT NOT ORDAINED*
††	*ORDAINED*
†††	*VERY ORDAINED*
††††	*ORDAINED WITH SWIMMING POOL*
†††††	*ORDAINED WITH SWIMMING POOL AND FRENCH CUISINE*
	*PARKING FACILITIES*
	*UNDERCOVER PARKING FACILITIES*
 5000	*PARTY BOOKINGS WITH NUMBER ACCEPTED, IN RESTAURANT*
LP	*LOCUST PLAGUE IN ALL ROOMS*
LC	*LEPER COLONY IN ALL ROOMS*
ALC	*À LA CARTE FASTS SERVED*
	*POPES WELCOME*
	*NOT SUITABLE FOR METHODISTS*
	*HOLY BOOK-ABLE IN ADVANCE*
	*MIRACLES AVAILABLE IN CERTAIN ROOMS*
	*CONTINENTAL BREAKFAST*
	*SHEPHERDS WELCOME*
	*MULTI-DENOMINATIONAL*

CD	*COLD DINNER ONLY ON SABBATH*
18	*18 HOLY GOLF COURSE ON PREMISES*
	NO NEIGHBOUR'S ASSES
163	*THE NEXT HYMN WILL BE NUMBER 163*
10	*LAST SUPPER 10 O'CLOCK*
i	*TOURIST INFORMATION CENTRE*
POP. 20,000	*POPULATION*
MD MON	*MARKET DAY*
	BRIDAL SUITE
	COACH PARTIES ACCEPTED
	COACH PARTIES ACCEPTED AND TURNED INTO WINE
20	*NUMBER OF CHURCHES*
MON	*CHOIR PRACTICE NIGHT*
MON	*UNDERWATER CHOIR PRACTICE NIGHT*
K	*KOSHER MENU AVAILABLE*
TUE	*BLESSING DAY*
	WAITERS CAN'T SET THE TABLE PROPERLY
P	*PRAY-AS-YOU-ENTER CAR PARK*
	BUNK BEDS IN ALL ROOMS (INCLUDING DINING ROOM)

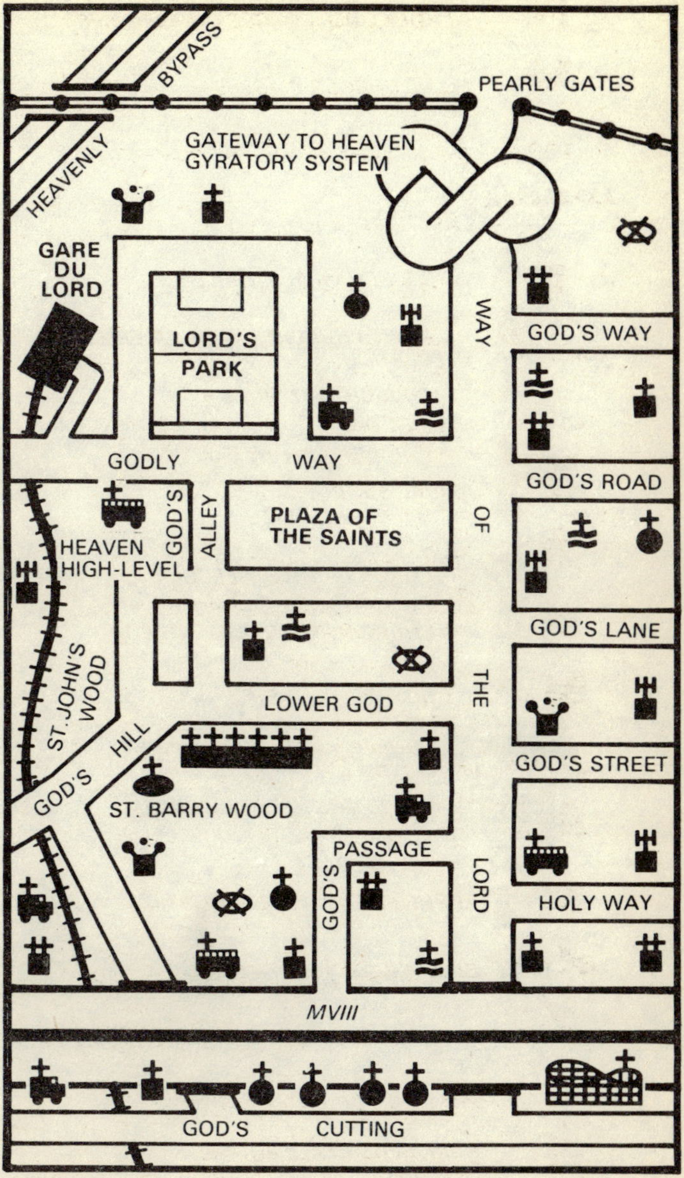
BYPASS
PEARLY GATES
HEAVENLY
GATEWAY TO HEAVEN
GYRATORY SYSTEM
GARE
DU
LORD
LORD'S
PARK
WAY
GOD'S WAY
GODLY
WAY
GOD'S ROAD
GOD'S
ALLEY
PLAZA OF
THE SAINTS
OF
HEAVEN
HIGH-LEVEL
GOD'S LANE
ST. JOHN'S
WOOD
THE
LOWER GOD
HILL
GOD'S STREET
GOD'S
ST. BARRY WOOD
PASSAGE
GOD'S
LORD
HOLY WAY
MVIII
GOD'S
CUTTING

 CHURCH WITH STEEPLE

 MORE CHURCHES WITH STEEPLES

 CHURCH WITH RUGBY

 CHURCH WITH TOWER

 DRIVE-IN CHURCH

 COACH PARTIES WELCOME

 CHURCH WITH SWIMMING POOL

 CHURCH WITH STEREO

 CHURCH WITH SUPERMARKET

 MIXED CHURCH AND FUNFAIR

 NO HALOES

 CHURCH WITH T.V.

 CHURCH WITH PING-PONG

ROAD SIGNS OF HEAVEN

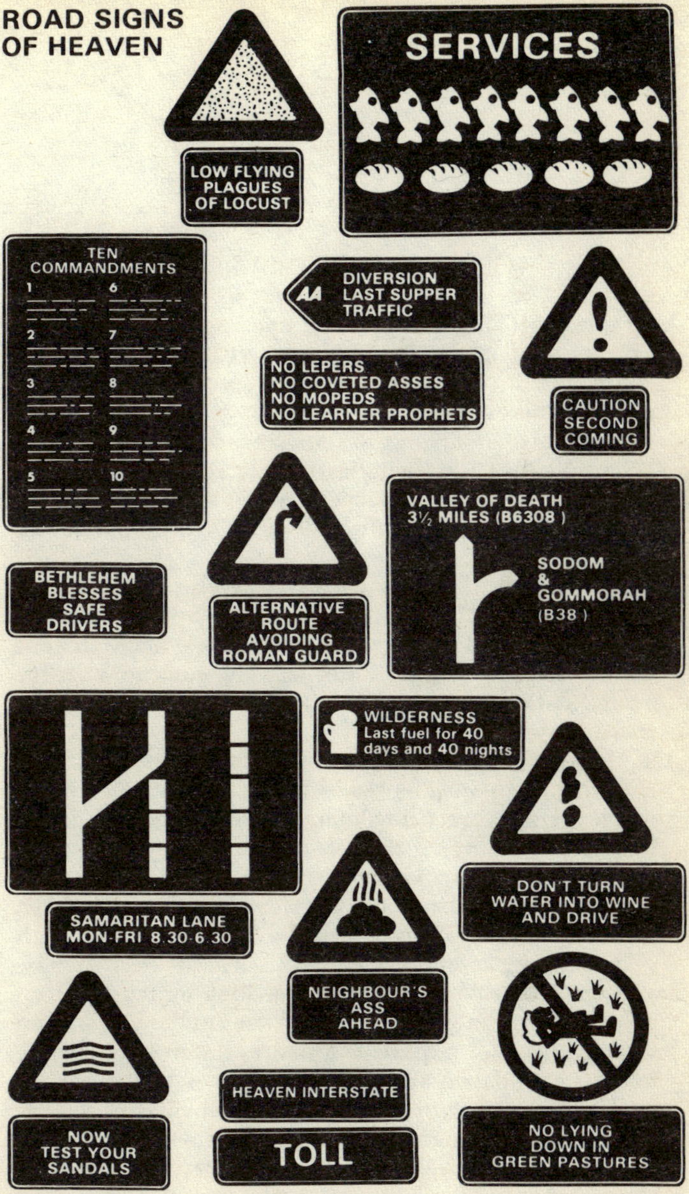

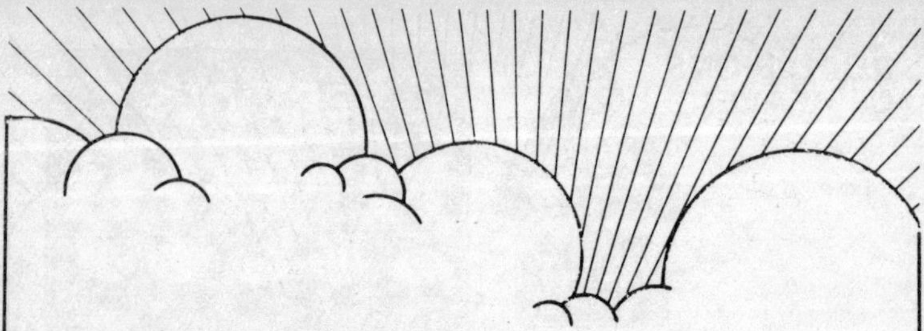

GENERAL INFORMATION

Agoraphobia (The fear of wide open spaces) Heaven's not a good place for sufferers from this common complaint. In very extreme cases specially constructed cells can be obtained. Most visitors find that they can overcome their anxiety by sticking close to walls and high buildings for their first few days. From this they move to cutting a few corners and in time they become accustomed to looking into the wide azure yonder and seeing for ever ... and ever.

Almighty (The) Visitors are always welcome (Tuesdays and Thursdays, 2.00 to 4.00 pm March–September). It is strongly advised that you book well in advance (current waiting list – 793 years). Alternatively, you can write for a cancellation which may reduce your waiting time to a mere six years.

Art Heaven is the art world's paradise. Indeed many of the world's greatest works of art were originally created in Heaven before being marketed on Earth as 'divine inspirations'. Among the most memorable works to be seen in the State Gallery are *Venus*, with arms, the complete set of Last meals (*Last Supper, Last Dinner, Last Tea, Last Cooked Breakfast, Last British Rail Sandwich*) and a rough pen-and-ink sketch entitled *Madonna and Twins*.

Banking In Heaven all banking is done by trust, which gives rise to the general term Trust Funds. Dealings in Goodwill do not require paperwork, statements, cheque books or embarrassing confrontations with bank managers. In Heaven your promise of Goodwill is as good as your word. Making a withdrawal in Heaven is as simple as saying, 'It's all right, I don't want a pay rise this year.

Give it to the government.' You just walk into your branch, or any other branch for that matter, and help yourself to as much Goodwill as you want. Even if you are tempted to fiddle the system, it wouldn't really matter. There's so much of everything, especially Goodwill, that no one would ever notice.

Baths Baths in Heaven are very popular. There is only one rule. You must not walk on the water while other people are swimming.

Chiropodists These are available in most towns. They perform a variety of services to the feet and anoint them simply for the pleasure they get from doing so. Naturally corns and bunions are simple ways of displaying suffering and forbearance. Consequently, there has been a growing demand for them in recent years and chiropodists do a roaring trade in fitting otherwise healthy feet with a variety of unpleasant growths and callouses.

Clouds/Cloud Hire After feet, clouds are the most common means of transport in Heaven. Few visitors arrive on their own clouds and since there is nothing to be gained from private cloud ownership, hire clouds have followed in the wake of the recent depression. To arrange for a cloud all you have to do is ring one of the many agencies listed in the directories: St Avis, St Godfrey Davis, Bleeding Hertz and St Salford of Van-Hire are the largest operators.

Cosmetics Though not strictly frowned upon in Heaven, cosmetics should always be worn with restraint. Here above all other places you will gain nothing from parading about with a face painted like the ceiling of the Sistine Chapel. Among the men in Heaven 'After-

Prayer' is a popular deodorant. Ladies prefer 'Apré-Bless' and 'Eau-de-Cologne-Cathedral'.

Dentists Dental problems disappear as soon as you pass through the Pearly Gates. Dentures are miraculously replaced by your former teeth and the Heavenly diet ensures that no further harm comes to your teeth. As a result there are no practising dentists in Heaven.

Dress Yes, you must. (See the later section on Vestments for full details.)

Electricity There is no electricity in Heaven. Any that is accidentally imported is disposed of by occasional flashes of lightning which return it to Earth. In Heaven electricity is replaced by a power-source seldom used on Earth – will-power. 'Have Faith Unto It And It will Be Seen To Work' is the maxim and all appliances that on Earth were worked by electricity are worked by will-power in Heaven. This unique technology does away with dangerous live wires and the risk of power failures. The only risk occurs when two people of conflicting will-powers try to use the same appliance at the same time. That can result in chaos. Fortunately occurrences like this are very rare.

Hangovers Hangovers as such don't exist in Heaven. However, excessive indulgence in milk and honey can lead to unpleasant consequences the following morning. The most popular remedy is a dose of St Andrew, which always provides a much needed breaking wind.

Hair Care Barbers are common in Heaven, but a visit to a barber's shop there is like nothing on Earth. A haircut means the same the Kingdom over, wavy golden hair with a full beard (unless you're a woman, in which case the beard is optional). For a place that prides itself on creativity this smacks of extreme conservatism. There is a compensation for this though. The level of conversation in a Heavenly barber's is a world apart from the platitudes and nonsense most of us are used to.

There's no talk of football, which, thank God, is banned in Heaven. There's no talk of the weather either since this is always the same and therefore makes an even more tedious topic of conversation than the weather on Earth. A barber's shop in Heaven offers much wider and deeper subjects to while away your time. You might find yourself asked to defend the money-lenders in the temple. You might be offered a rendering from one of the gospels in Coptic. You could well stumble across a heated argument over the Alternative Service Book into which you find yourself irresistibly dragged. A visit to the barber's shop in Heaven gives you more than a haircut; it introduces you to a whole new philosophy and outlook as well.

Jokes Care should be taken in telling jokes in Heaven. The locals are quick to take offence. Diligent research has so far produced only three jokes that would meet all the requirements of decency and respectability demanded in Heaven. These are so boring that there's no point in telling them anyway.

Kissing Other than popes' toes, kissing is frowned upon in Heaven.

Laundry Even the most dazzling vestments require the occasional wash and in Heaven there's no shortage of Selfless-Service Laundromats and Dry-Purgers to help clean you up. Their terms are reasonable and the service is always quick and efficient.

Law (The) The national concern with honesty, fairness

and justice made any form of legal system obsolete centuries ago. As a result all laws were repealed and the police force was disbanded. The SPG group has come in for some criticism recently. It was felt in some Heavenly quarters that the Salvation, Peace and Goodness force were exceeding the powers of their brief. But since they have always been set aside from the general arm of the law, their services are still called upon.

News News is generally the province of the prophets who receive it on average about six weeks before any given event actually takes place. (There is a phrase in Heaven that goes, 'There's nothing so dead as next month's news' and every prophet tries to be the first with the tidings.) Most news agencies are run by the prophets who control the reporting of all hot news stories from the universe and beyond. If you want to keep in touch with events at home and abroad the most widely read daily and weekly papers are *The Son, The Sabbath Times, The Herald Tribute, Next Sunday Express, The Guardian Angle* (sic) and *News of the Heaven.*

Parking When parking your cloud always try to use the cloud meters provided. Long stay cloud-parks are signposted in all major centres. Use these to prevent your clouds from evaporating.

Pets/Domestic Animals Animals are not strictly allowed into Heaven either as pets or beasts of burden. However, particularly worthy animals (Lassie, Muffin The Mule, Rin Tin Tin, Trigger, for example) can get there in their own right and the immigration authorities turn a blind eye to a wide range of other animals who attempt to get past the Pearly Gates.

Pharmacy Pharmacists exist in Heaven to provide reassurance to hypochondriacs who can't get used to being fit and healthy for eternity. The largest chain of retailers is owned by the Moses group whose motto is 'Keep taking the tablets'.

Queries Try YHA first of all. If they can't help you, go to The Heavenly Information Office, or call in at any of their branches displaying this sign:

Rules of the Air Angels of the Lord obey the normal laws of the road and fly to the right. This applies to clouds too. Clouds must also carry conventional navigational and warning lights. There are no speed restrictions in Heaven, but we respectfully remind you once again that he who is first shall be last and vice versa.

Services Morning Services, Evening Services, Afternoon Services, Family Services, even Lunchtime and Breakfast Services – Heaven has a Service to suit everyone night and day. See the local press for full details.

Shopping To be perfectly candid, Heaven has never been an exciting shopping centre. Pleasures of the flesh are unheard of and other mortal comforts are a bit thin on the ground. Those prepared to poke around the back streets of Heaven sometimes turn up remarkable bargains. But as everywhere 'abroad' there are pitfalls waiting for the unwary visitor. Be suspicious of the man who tries to sell you anything 'for thirty talents of silver'.

Watch out too for the hawkers who offer miracle meals (five loaves and two fishes are the popular ingredients, which the hawker will insist can feed a multitude, usually taken to mean five thousand). Bargaining is not practised in Heaven. The Lord giveth and the Lord taketh away; the prices are fixed, though subject to tax.

Sickness Fast miracles are available through the NHS (National Healer Service). In the event of sickness or ill-health, send forth thine prayers (preferably before 9.30 am on the day you want the Healer to call) and you will receive a wondrous visitation. For less troublesome complaints you should attend one of the regular mass cleansing ceremonies.

Sunday Schools Everyone in Heaven attends Sunday schools, even adults. What's more they don't restrict their attendance to Sundays. Sunday schools are held on every day of the week.

Time Heaven time is Time Immemorial. This is the equivalent of GMT minus 1 aeon.

Transport In addition to the methods mentioned previously (feet and clouds) other modes of travel also exist in Heaven. Spontaneous levitation, jogging, crawling (very popular with repentomaniacs) and asses are frequently used. The use of wings is restricted to Angels.

Visitors' Book Visitors who wish to may sign the visitors' book as they enter the Kingdom. Previous visitors' books containing the names of some of the most illustrious figures in history can be seen in The Kingdom of Heaven Museum. A recent change to the visitors' book has been the dropping of the Comments column. It was found that visitors were taking so long to express their delight and in many cases relief at being admitted to Heaven that they were each filling three or four books with Comments.

Water For once you need have no fear about drinking local water. Heavenly water is as pure as pure can be. It is piped into every home and other building in the land. It has the additional advantage of being self-purifying, which means that one tankful will last a lifetime – and with the help of astute water collection it frequently does.

Wind (ethereal) Pharmacists will be able to provide a suitable medicament.

Zithers Take the same medicament as prescribed for wind.

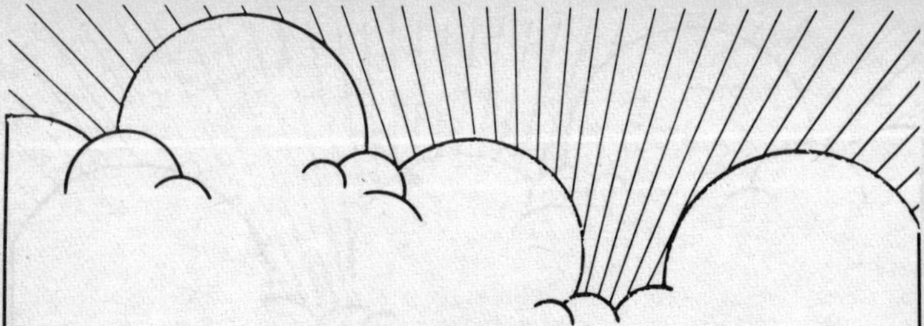

A to Z of HEAVEN

HISTORY OF HEAVEN

The earliest traces of Heavenly habitation have long since disappeared. It can only be assumed that Heaven somehow avoided the Palaeolithic era which marks the earliest datable time for most other civilizations, since no evidence of this type of culture has yet been discovered. Nor is there any record in the archives of exactly when Heaven was established. Taking the official line which states that God is the founder of the Universe, then Heaven must have been created at the same time, that is to say one aeon ago.

There may always have been a Heaven, but it was only brought into use during comparatively recent times – the period covered by the Bible. Until then the place remained virtually empty with a skeleton staff of maintenance men and cleaners. Inevitably this thesis raises certain awkward questions. Are we to imply from this that no one else from the universe is allowed into 'our' Heaven? Is it that other beings from outside are not 'good' enough to gain admittance?

The answer to both of these is again disappointingly that we don't know. What's more God himself is far from forthcoming on the subject. One theory states that other beings from the universe are equally as good as those from Earth, it's just that they're good in other ways, ways that are incompatible with our own. And bearing in mind that all visitors have just experienced the biggest culture shock of their lives it does seem a bit hard to subject them to another whopper as soon as they step inside the Pearly Gates. Coming to terms with the other world is demanding enough without having to get used to rubbing shoulders with disembodied Martians and souls from Alpha Centauri. That at least is the theory – how far you take it is very much up to you.

In contrast to the early history, which, as we have explained, is lost in the mists of eternity, recent history in Heaven has been exhaustively documented in numerous scholarly works. The present metropolis was constructed at about 200 BC in anticipation of the great influx of new souls that was expected after the birth of Christianity. Since then it has been in a state of almost constant expansion as the immigration numbers have swollen.

This rapid growth had a knock-on effect itself. As new souls arrived, bringing with them new experiences and new life-styles, the Lord tried to incorporate these into his building and planning programmes so that no one should feel neglected or homesick. This policy may come as a surprise, as all these ideas originated with the Lord anyway. But in a sense, by adopting this course, he is able to undertake some valuable market research on Earth before actually taking the steps of introducing a new concept into Heaven. If there's no demand for his product on Earth, he can be certain that it won't be missed in Heaven. This policy also ensures that Heaven is free of the many embarrassing failures and flops that form part of Earth's uneasy evolution. Heaven is perfect and the Lord is determined to keep it that way. By the time anything is introduced into the home market you can guarantee that it's been well and truly tested elsewhere.

If you've ever wondered how Heaven has succeeded in maintaining its overriding superiority in everything, here's your answer: by guaranteeing a one hundred per cent success rate with new developments and by knowing precisely what the market needs at any given time, Heaven has been able to remain far ahead of its nearest rivals in terms of standard of living and quality of life. Of course, Heaven is a totally protected market itself. As we've mentioned earlier we bring nothing into the world (Earth) and we take nothing out. With trade barriers like these Heaven is fully protected from market penetration, while its own export drive is limitless. Little wonder the Lord goes to bed each night a happy man.

A–Z OF HEAVEN

It would be an arrogant claim to assert that everything to do with Heaven could be confined within a book of this scale. But there are a number of interesting and important topics which we feel any prospective visitor would be well advised to acquaint himself or herself with. In the following pages we hope you will delve a little below the surface of the land of milk and honey.

Angels

One of the most dramatic differences between life in Heaven and that on Earth is the hierarchical system that still governs Heavenly society. This is manifested most obviously in the presence of angels.

Angels can be easily identified by their white raiment and purer-than-white demeanour. They also have large pointed wings. Angels are noteworthy too for the ease with which they appear to float for long periods in the Heavens. There is no apparent sign of strain, no perspiring effort. All is ease and comfort with them. Indeed angels never sweat; that is one of their privileges. It stands to reason that it wouldn't do to see the messengers of the Lord parading about with unsightly underwing stains, or worse still, sanctified body odour.

As we've hinted earlier, angel etiquette dictates that visitors should not attempt to approach or speak to them. They have a job to do, like the Horse Guards on duty in London, so they won't thank you for distracting them. On the other hand you can take it for granted that they are always watching over you to make sure that you don't come to any harm.

Off-duty angels tend to keep themselves to themselves, rather like police officers or prison warders. This is the reason why you will seldom run into an off-duty angel socially. If you should happen to come across one, your best policy will be to adopt a deferential air and get out of their way as fast as possible, as you would on running your trolley into the Pope in Sainsbury's.

One up from angels come the archangels. These are about the size of a largish semi and are dressed similarly to a bishop on Earth, though they do not wear mitres when they are flying. The arrival of an archangel is heralded by the sound of the Holy Choir in Vestibule (broadcast in stereo) and a parting of the clouds. The first time you bear witness to events like these you should immediately cast yourself to the ground. By all means throw yourself into the part, but draw the line at renting your garments in twain. This is vehemently discouraged in Heaven.

Unlike angels, archangels will address you directly. You have no need to worry though. The level of conversation is no more demanding than that with a member of the royal family. In reply to questions like 'Are you feeling well?', 'Have you still got a cold?' and 'Hey mister, want to buy postcards, very cheap?' you are only required to mutter your answer in a deferential manner and leave it at that. All answers should be positive.

For those contemplating becoming angels themselves there's no time like the present to start. Nothing short of a life of penitence is required. The first position you're likely to be offered is that of non-commissioned angel. This alone necessitates passing a lengthy examination on biblical texts and moral theology, followed by a practical test in which you have to construct a giant act of magnanimity using a rope, a box and two long pieces of wood. The final test is an angelic assault course – a terrifying array of temptations from free Russian caviar for life to a suite of your own in the Las Vegas hotel of your choice. It goes without saying that you will be expected to resist each of these without question.

Subsequently successful candidates – who then become known as cherubs – spend six months at the Wilderness Training Centre where the drop-out rate is an alarming 99.9997 per cent. However, those who make it are enrolled as fully fledged angels and take part in the spectacular 'float past' at which newly enrolled angels are given their wings for the first time.

Blessing

'Him that blesses last blesses longest' is an old Heavenly saying as applicable today as it has always been. Heaven is a land of blessings and they have become inextricably intertwined with the fabric of daily life.

It would be folly to list here all the heavenly moments when one might be expected to bless or be blessed. Making breakfast, for instance, requires no fewer than seventeen separate blessings. Pouring a gin and tonic at certain times of the day can raise as many as twenty. Blessings are expected at bathtime, at the meal table, when dressing, when out walking or floating, indeed in every facet of daily life. The modern tendency to eat cold food has done away with many of the Heavenly blessings associated with cooking. It also means that spirits are no longer forced to eat unappetising, lukewarm food congealed on their plates because they've spent over half the meal saying grace and blessing each other.

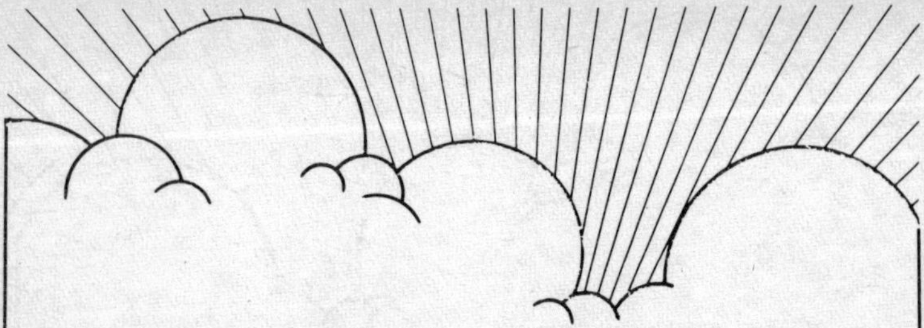

Meeting friends in the street involves an elaborate interchange of blessings and greetings which are bandied about between one speaker and the other like balls in an impressive rally at tennis. If two groups of people happen to meet it's as well to resign yourself to giving up the purpose of your walk. You'll probably be there all day.

It's not surprising that such a situation should give rise to a burgeoning industry based on the principle 'Bless now and pray later'. This is a system widely practised in Heaven in which subscribers cut their blessings to a minimum on the understanding that they will make up the lost blessings when they are next praying at leisure.

There is a similar scheme operated by the Count Your Blessings Bank, which has become increasingly attractive over the years. All you do is store up advance blessings, making deposits when you have time to spare, so that you can trade them off in the future. This is an ideal scheme for those who can't afford to spend the greater part of their day down on their knees making up for past blessings, but who are able to bless in advance, by careful forward thinking.

One of the more curious aspects of the use of blessings in Heaven is that blessings are negotiable. A house or similar property may be traded on the strength of the number of times that someone has said 'Bless this house'. Similarly secondhand clouds attain value according to the number of times they have been blessed. For example, a recent advertisement appearing in one of the Heavenly dailies read: '*For Sale:* one cloud, 256,000 blessings from new'. This frame of mind works in complete contrast to that on Earth of course, where the normal purchaser is looking for the minimum as opposed to the maximum amount of use in any purchase.

As a general rule the safest policy to adopt when in Heaven is 'When in doubt – bless'. Be like the raw recruit who's told to salute anything that moves. You'll find you won't go far wrong.

Clouds

To visitors from Earth, notably those from the British Isles, clouds and the intense preoccupation with them in Heaven will strike a familiar homely chord. For clouds are to the souls in Heaven, what the weather is to the British. Comments like, 'It looks like Cirrostratus again today' or 'It's been the Cumulusest March for forty-one years', or even 'It's been Nimbusing down all bloody day!' may be heard in any bar, or on any street in Heaven. Cloud forecasts are carried after every news bulletin on television too.

Familiarity may breed contempt on Earth, but in Heaven familiarity with the clouds is a *sine qua non*. Get in as much practise at cloud spotting as you can before you make your trip. Apart from anything else an ability to identify the clouds will make the journey itself a lot more interesting. Some take this to extremes and walk round with their heads permanently pointing skywards. They devise home-made clamps that lock their heads at an angle of forty-five degrees (metal coat hangers are the most popular materials). There are dangers in this policy, so be careful. Many zealots have found themselves partially crippled with cricked necks and many more have driven into ditches as they attempt to negotiate their first bends in the car.

Clouds, like camels, require a riding skill of their own. It was no accident that the earliest cloud riders came from the Middle East where magic carpet transport has long been in vogue. It has to be said that clouds are essentially very uncomfortable. What we may regard in our ignorance as design faults are in fact part of a carefully thought out penitence policy.

Clouds are cold, wet and clammy and sitting on them is tantamount to sitting on piles of soggy cotton wool. Clearly no ordinary mortal can be expected to sit on a mass of insubstantial dampness and relish the experience. This is part of the divine secret. It also explains the overbearing seriousness and air of stoicism that many cloud riders exude.

Similarly cloud maintenance is not a skill that is easily acquired. Every visitor to Heaven has to face the fact that if he or she isn't possessed of a saintly countenance and doesn't like water, then cloud ownership is not for them. The major hazards face clouds and their owners – precipitation and evaporation. Experience has shown that the most effective ways to guard against these is to keep moving. This at least helps to stave off the fateful day when the cloud finally disintegrates.

Although most experts advise cloud owners to keep on the move, clouds are not built for speed. Not only are cloud owners expected to maintain a certain decorum, to which zipping through the airways is anything but conducive, but clouds themselves are not built for fast travel. Even though it may seem sensible to streamline clouds, by trimming off some of the unnecessary lumps and bulges, aerodynamics play no part in divine aesthetics. In the same way cloud topiary is frowned upon as being both *nouveau riche* and wildly ostentatious. It simply isn't done to go floating about Heaven on a cloud that looks like an airborne garden from Worthing. No matter how unpleasant a cloud may remain to its owner, it is there to be suffered in dignified silence, not to be flaunted as a masterpiece of undignified vulgarity.

You might be forgiven for construing from the above that cloud ownership has little to recommend it. You would be wrong. The rewards of cloud ownership are in Heaven alone. Cloud owners enjoy a special relationship with the Lord ('Nearer my God to thee' is their maxim). Those able to suffer the discomfort and obvious inconvenience of cloud travel score high penitence points, which explains the ever growing list of those waiting for their cloud driving tests.

Apart from the important social cachet associated with clouds, they are also remarkably safe to travel on. Clouds provide excellent all-round vision and their spongy surfaces act as highly effective shock-absorbers. So safe are clouds that the first fatality from a cloud impact has yet to be recorded. This goes some way to explaining why saints and angels are never depicted wearing safety-belts.

It is also more or less impossible to fall off a cloud without a great deal of effort. Should you try to crawl towards the edge while in flight, the tendency is for the whole cloud to start to revolve beneath you as you shift your weight. The result of this is that you never actually reach the edge. Instead you remain rather like a seal at the circus perched on top of a revolving ball.

The last but in many owners' opinions the most important reason for having a cloud of your own is its undoubted value as a status symbol. Spending eternity floating about on what feels like a well-used, giant-sized nappy, or a vast leaking water-bed, may not be everyone's idea of Heaven, but like Hindu fakirs who undergo appalling privations and discomforts, it gains eternal respect, which is worth a lot in the hereafter.

Prospective cloud owners can get full details and free advice about clouds from the Cloud Owners' Club (COC) on arrival in Heaven. Their office is clearly signposted from the Pearly Gates, but as you'd expect it's always on the move. Happy Floating!

Day of Judgement, The

The Day of Judgement has long been a source of fascination for most members of the universe. In a nutshell it's the grand totting up, when all our sins and trespasses are balanced against our good deeds. Those who end up in credit get a one-way ticket to Heaven. The others get a free pass to Hell, Heaven help them.

The date of the Day of Judgement hasn't been announced yet and in the light of past experience it probably never will be. We'll just wake up one morning to find a large banner in the sky explaining that today's the chosen day. Vague and inconclusive as this may appear, there is a method in the Lord's apparent madness. Since none of us knows when we're going to be called forth to give an account of our lives, it's naturally in our own interests to keep our slates as clean as possible.

The only principal difference between settling our score with the Lord before Judgement Day and settling it on the day itself is that in the first case you'll be interviewed by St Peter, or more likely one of his team. Whereas on Judgement Day the Lord himself takes the chair. And that's a very different kettle of fish. At the Pearly Gates you are at least given a chance to air your own feelings on the subject of your life and destiny. On the Day of Judgement, you're not. On that day the whole of mankind is judged collectively and it's too bad if you happen to be tarred with your neighbour's brush, particularly if your neighbour has spent his years on Earth making a bomb from screening blue movies and selling booze illicitly to the whole district.

As no one knows what form the Day of Judgement will take either, that also hangs over everyone's head like a sword of Damocles. The official line is 'Arrangements will be made in due course.'

Where the Day of Judgement actively affects those in Heaven is in their compassionate concern for those left on Earth. Realising as they do, the terrible consequences awaiting so many of Earth's citizens from trades union leaders to members of the hunting fraternity, they are constantly at pains to try to persuade us to repent before it is too late. Sad to say, so much of what they say falls on deaf ears, though they'll be the ears that will hear Hell's monotonous drumming only too clearly.

The only ones who won't be affected by the Day of Judgement are those in Hell already. It's a mistake to believe in a divine parole, once there, you're there for good (or evil, as it happens). So warning people in Hell about the Day of Judgement is like telling a man serving a sentence of life imprisonment that a friend of yours might be arrested at some time in the future for shoplifting. If you've already booked your ride to Hell, the Day of Judgement is one thing that you needn't be bothered about.

Equality

Everyone is equal in the eyes of the Lord and equality governs every facet of Heavenly life. As one commentator wryly expressed it, 'It's a riot of Marxism – only without the politics.' Laudable as this policy may appear at first sight, it is not without its pitfalls. Social and business interchange are certainly placed on very shaky ground by it. No-one in Heaven knows to whom they should offer their seat in a cloud, or even if they should offer it at all. Worker's aren't sure whether they should pay lip service to their bosses, or whether their bosses should pay lip service to them. Taking this a stage further, no one is really certain who is boss and who is worker, and even though very little has to be done in Heaven to make the economy tick, there are all the large public works undertakings that require a modicum of organisation and control.

The net result of this egalitarianism is that nothing gets done without a certain amount of pressure. Lines and approaches like, 'I know that we're equal, but ...' go part of the way towards a more practical working relationship, but as usual it falls to the Lord's lot to get things moving. For he is the one being in Heaven who is anything but equal. He gets things done and people know about it too. This had the added effect that the Lord's works become even more wondrous, since they're about the only ones that ever get done. It's a grave mistake to take this magnanimity for granted. The Lord doesn't take kindly to being pestered every time that there's something wrong with the plumbing or the cloud is due for a major service. *But* if there really is a crisis and something needs doing, don't hesitate to seek divine intervention.

Fasts

Among the many new and intriguing pastimes that greet any visitor to Heaven is the practice of fasting. Fasts are part and parcel of daily life in Heaven and they cause no real fuss, though it is customary to warn your hostess in advance that you are on a fast lest she should take offence when you leave her food untouched.

Fasting is a simple and easy pastime that requires no special skills, training, or equipment. For those who want to make their fasts just a little bit more of a test of their will-power, there are empty food packets and tins on the market.

On average fasts in Heaven last for no more than a couple of days and they usually take place near the beginning of the week. No one wants a secondary fast forced upon them when they find that the food shops are shut at the week-end. In recent years an interesting variant of the traditional fast has been gaining popularity, though it has still to receive official recognition. This is the quickie fast which never lasts more than twenty minutes. A quickie fast is simple, time-saving and convenient. You can arrange one at a moment's notice to coincide with a milk and honey break or a journey home from work.

Even more attractive is the part-time fast, in which the participant regularly fasts between meals. This type of fast allows one to maintain a fast almost indefinitely.

The problem with fasting, even with these modern, easy-term fasts, is that it can't always be fitted in to a busy Heavenly timetable. But there's an answer to this as well – fasting by proxy. If you're unable or unwilling to fast yourself, fasting by proxy gives you all the satisfaction of a fully fledged fast, with none of the discomfort. All you have to do is nominate the faster of your choice and let him or her get on with it. The beauty of this scheme is that it follows the maxim that it is better to give than to receive to the letter.

One final point should be made about fasting. Fasting on

an empty stomach is very unwise. Those who practise this are liable to end up with unpleasant stomach cramps and a frustrated ambition.

God

Architect, statesman, diplomat, administrator and supreme being of the universe, God defies description. Suffice it to say that without him there would be no Heaven. (Some argue that there'd also be no Hell, but that's another matter.) For years people have looked for flaws in God. They have looked for chinks in the armour. They have searched for skeletons in the cupboard. Psychologists have raised doubts about possible schizophrenia, on the grounds of the three-in-one syndrome. But so far none of these researches has succeeded in casting the slightest shadow over God's impeccable nature.

On Earth perhaps, such a personality would become more than a little trying. Even in an age where excellence is universally applauded God would quickly get on everyone's nerves because he is quite simply the best at everything. In Heaven this is not the case. Baser human feelings of greed, envy, jealousy and covetousness have no place in the world above. Far from despising the concept of a universal excellence embodied in one being this is praised to the skies, a trend which in past millennia has even filtered down to some sections of Earthly society, albeit in a diluted form.

But God isn't good at everything. There are some aspects of life, as practised on Earth in which he falls short of the mark. God isn't good at doing wrong. He's not much use when it comes to sinning. He completely misunderstands the first principles of being rude. He can't get angry over petty issues and when it comes to blindless aggression he's a complete non-starter. So taken on this level God is something of a disaster.

That God is industrious no one can deny and who would begrudge a day off to the being who created the Earth in six days? (Possibly skunks and eskimoes, who feel that they've had a raw deal, but it's almost impossible to satisfy everyone.) 'God's work is never done', is his tireless motto and this relentless champion of the poor, the needy and the oppressed never spares himself when it comes to helping others or working for the good of all.

Conservative in dress and manner – he's seldom seen in anything but snowy-white vestments – God cuts a rather lonely figure in the world above. Adored by all, worshipped and glorified he may be, but apart from his son, he has no immediate family. Many have anticipated the time when he eventually relinquishes the heavy burden he has borne for so long, allowing younger shoulders to carry the cross he bears. However, there are no signs of his pending abdication and we very much doubt if there will be any in the foreseeable future. God has gone on record several times claiming that his work is eternal, and who are we to argue with him about that? Certainly no one could question his unique talent for carrying out this super-human task. Our only duty is to make his job as easy and pleasant as we can. After all, it's for our benefit that he is working.

For details of visiting God see Almighty (The) under General Information.

Harps

No book on Heaven would be complete without a mention

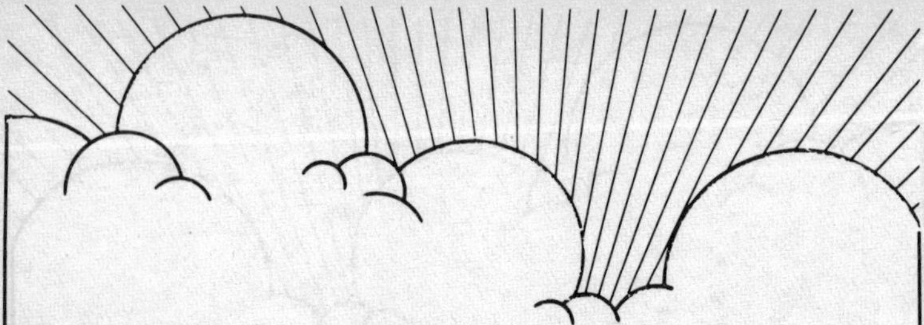

of the harp. In Heaven it is everyone's favourite musical instrument, and because so few qualified harp players arrive in Heaven each year there is a well-established tradition of training novices from scratch. Even the visitor with no previous experience will find a forum in which to learn and enjoy his instrument with no awkwardness or embarrassment.

The tradition of harp playing in Heaven has given rise to a bewildering variety of different styles of harp from which players can choose. The classic is still the 'Gabriel' (named after the inventor) and you could do far worse than settle for a good second-hand model to begin with. The 'Gabriel' is everything you would expect from an easily portable harp. It is triangular in shape, conventionally sized and designed with an attractive carved wooden frame. It has been described as the Volkswagen of harps and is every bit as enduring.

Don't let conventions govern your choice though. Harps are for pleasure and with a wide variety to choose from for once in eternity you can afford to indulge yourself. Harps come in all shapes and sizes. They can be large or small, round or square. They can be made of wood, steel, plastic, ivory, gold, cardboard or even fibre glass and they can be provided in any colour you choose. Even the number of strings is unfixed (as indeed are a number of the strings themselves in the cheaper models). The minimum number, to qualify as a harp, is one. Several of these mono-stringed harps are available for the casual player who looks on his harp as more of a social prop than a serious musical instrument. At the other end of the scale is the omni-harp with a record 352,719 strings at the last count.

As might be expected from an instrument with such

universal popularity there are any number of ways in which the harp can be played. Harps can be played on your back, on your side, on someone else's side, in bed, or in the case of the aqua-harp, underwater.

A further reason for the harp's popularity is the ease with which even the novice can produce an acceptable sound. Simply running one's fingers across the strings can produce a most agreeable noise, which to the untrained ear sounds pretty authentic, and as we've already mentioned, there aren't that many trained ears in Heaven. The only other prerequisite is the adoption of a melancholy expression which distinguishes the serious harp player from the social player. Once you have mastered these two basic skills you are ready to start playing.

Most players quickly want to graduate to using both hands and this can be accomplished with the minimum of effort. Try running both hands over the strings in a graceful, sylphlike manner, first one way and then the other. The easiest movement is the large circle, which you describe over the full area of the strings, first on one side and then on the other. From the circular movement you can graduate to the figure of '8' and then to the 'S' shape, which is half the '8'. Be sure all the time to maintain the same melancholy expression.

After perfecting the rudimentary movements you may find that you start to recognise certain chords and you may even be able to hit these deliberately as your technique improves. Whatever your basic skills you ought now to be in the position of being able to cobble together a fairly respectable piece of Heavenly music which looks and sounds as if you know what you are trying to achieve. This is the time to introduce the third ingredient into your performance: the so-called choral illustration, which usually, and in the case of beginners always, takes the form of relentless moans and wails.

Playing with other people is a test of patience and frequently of friendship. Since it is highly unlikely that you will ever be fortunate enough to hit the same notes simultaneously the only way to play acceptably as a group is for one player to begin and then to take it in turns to carry on the piece. During the periods when you are not playing yourself it is quite in order to continue to look melancholic. More often than not you will choose to look like that anyway.

The sound of the harp generally induces a state of complete tranquillity for both performer and audience, which is of course singularly appropriate for a place like Heaven. Unfortunately, for all its excellent qualities harp playing can easily become addictive. Harper's Anonymous exists to help those who have found it too much for them.

Haloes

One of the most perplexing mysteries in Heaven is the importance attached to haloes. To all intents and purposes haloes are clumsy, heavy, difficult to wear and provide little if any protection against the elements. But haloes and Heaven go together and no visitor to Heaven can begin to feel at home unless he or she is wearing one.

Haloes are issued in Heaven like gym shorts in the army and little is to be gained from complaining if yours is too big or too small. Astute swapping later on can improve matters, but to be honest it is seldom worth the effort. Few people notice the halo since everyone in Heaven wears them. Indeed you're far more likely to stand out in the crowd if you are wearing one that fits perfectly. That implies that you've been spending too much time halo-swapping.

In the last few centuries there has been a growing tendency in Heaven to carry a spare halo. Again this is little more than a status symbol of questionable virtue and one that is much frowned upon by the powers that be.

All halo owners are well advised to take a few precautions in maintaining their haloes. Washing in warm water, for example, can distort haloes alarmingly. At best they emerge from the wash as ovals; at worst they come out looking like failed Henry Moores. The safest treatment for a soiled halo is a light sponge with holy water. If the stain proves to be too stubborn for this then it is best to have the halo dry cleaned. You should be careful about this too as the dry cleaners in Heaven are notorious for spreading malicious tidings and they're not above leaking whose haloes are the dirtiest which can have damaging consequences for some even innocent souls.

Recently haloes made from man-made fibres have become commonplace in Heaven; the ones made from nylon and polyester being the most prevalent. These are washable and remarkably sturdy. Their only drawback is that they do encourage one to sweat in warm weather which in turn can make the halo itself slippery and difficult to keep in place. Man-made fibre haloes also tend to be a bit shiny, especially in bright sunshine. While you may think that a sparkling halo is exactly what you need to cut a dash in Heaven you'd be sadly mistaken. For one thing only angels are allowed flashing haloes and for another the flashes from a halo can so easily be mistaken for illicit communication by Morse code that many an innocent victim has had some fast talking to do when hauled up in front of the Lord on a charge of spreading false prophecies.

All haloes are made to be worn and used, and a well-cared-for halo will repay its owner with years of trouble-free service. The principles for looking after a halo will come naturally to all who have experience of pressing flowers or keeping tennis rackets.

Your halo should always be stored flat, away from direct heat or sunlight and out of the reach of cherubs. If placed between two sheets of white paper haloes can be protected from creasing and dirt. Don't fall into the error of using newspaper for this purpose. Nothing is more embarrassing than wearing a halo with next week's news printed all over it.

One investment which many halo wearers find worth its weight in Goodwill is the Halo Ring. This adaptable tool resembling a flower press is presprung to the shape of your head (the shop from which you buy it will happily do this for you at no extra cost). Not only will the Halo Ring keep your halo neat and flat; it also includes an ingenious warning device that sounds the alarm as soon as it senses that your halo is starting to shift from the classically accepted lines in which it is held. The Halo Ring has a further point to recommend it. It prevents you from indulging in the most vulgar of practices, namely hanging your halo on a clothes peg.

Since the 1960s there has been a growing demand for new-wave haloes. This has been championed by a small, vociferous group who want greater liberalism in haloes and their use. This movement has introduced the controversial use of colour in their halo designs. Polychromatic haloes, psychedelic haloes, haloes with Paisley patterns and even haloes with pictures of the late President Kennedy and the Pope have appeared in Heaven. Haloes carrying flashing neon advertisements have been banned by the authorities – a move which was universally applauded. Likewise, the irreverent use of haloes as frisbees among some of the younger visitors was quickly stamped out and many of the culprits were deprived of their haloes for periods of up to five millennia.

At the risk of appearing to sound discriminatory we feel that we must also warn prospective visitors against succumbing to the temptation of wearing nationally identifiable haloes like the Australian halo with corks and bottle-openers hanging from strings, or the South American halo with a wide brim-like sombrero. Innocent as these may appear to be they do go against the essential spirit of Heaven. The climate and conditions do not require them and if the classical halo was good enough for the saints, it is certainly good enough for the run-of-the-mill visitor.

Wear a halo by all means but wear it correctly and wear it with pride. You'll have worked hard enough to get it after all!

Infinity

Of all the observations and remarks that are fed back to us from visitors the one overriding complaint is about infinity. This is understandable. Infinity is a difficult concept for the terrestrial mind to grasp. But Heaven and infinity go hand in hand, you can't have one without having the other.

In Heaven time is infinite; space is infinite; life (or afterlife) is infinite; everything around you is infinite.

While this removes the immediate pressures that most have come to accept as being commensurate with *being*, it also introduces problems and anxieties that are just as challenging and demanding. Love, peace and understanding may go on for ever, but so does the ceaseless quest for knowledge. By the same token an infinity filled with praying, fasting, playing the harp and floating about on clouds may dampen some of the initial enthusiasm for staying in Heaven.

All we can say in defence of infinity is that it is a well-proven policy which has not failed the divine purpose in all the years that it has been in force. It is impossible to try to imagine infinity, but that is exactly the Almighty's purpose. Were we able to comprehend infinity, one of the greatest mysteries of Heaven would be exposed. As it is, none of us knows the meaning of infinity until we step inside the Pearly Gates. That's the way the Lord wants it to remain and, as he's omnipotent, infinity is likely to remain a mystery for as long as time itself.

Jealousy

Jealousy may seem a curious subject to be discussed in a book about Heaven, but as so much of our life on Earth is governed by it, we can't avoid mentioning it here. Happily, jealousy, along with every other human vice, is left outside the Pearly Gates. As soon as you step inside a giant cloud of contentment envelopes you like the flocks of pigeons in St Mark's square in Venice. This has a wonderful purgative effect. It takes away the desire to beat the living daylights out of every other Saul, Luke and Matthew and replaces it with a sense of universal love and peace that admittedly takes some getting used to.

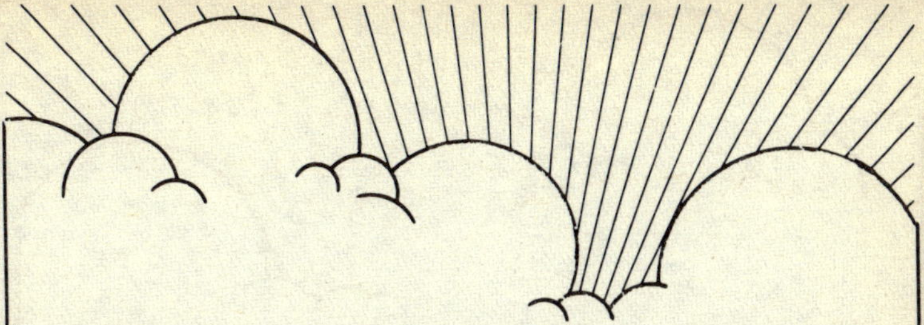

Many potential visitors rightly feel drawn to the idea of eschewing jealousy while they are still on Earth, but sad to say their efforts are poorly rewarded. The human spirit is too deeply engrained with the vice to give it up willingly and quite honestly it's pointless to start a personal crusade. You're far better off leading your own life and allowing others to lead theirs. It's disheartening but true that none of us is going to be able to put right the damage that was done in the Garden of Eden all those years ago.

Knowledge

Having said earlier that knowledge is an infinite study, we must dispel any doubts that its pursuit is pointless. This is not the case at all. Knowledge springs from God's eternal bosom and às God is all-seeing and all-doing the breadth of his knowledge is enormous. That said, it must be pointed out that in terms of earthly knowledge, the intellectual skills of the average soul are enormous too. Take for example the equation:

$$\frac{PQ^{r} + (ZN \times XX \times q)^{z} + 1}{p+b+c+9-45^{2} \times \frac{1}{2}} = \frac{(QRTSILODPMP1)^{2/3}}{z}$$

This appeared in a recent Heavenly O-level paper. There can't be many on Earth who would be able to answer that with the facility of the cherubs who each received an 'A' for their work.

Heaven has been described as 'an intellectual orgy', 'a total cerebral blow-out' and 'a bean-fast for the brain'. While we beg to differ with the terminology perhaps, the sentiment it embodies is undeniably valid. Heaven is a rich and stimulating mental experience that instantly transforms the theory of relativity to the level of comprehending a bingo card and makes it possible for most souls to understand their tax returns and insurance policies.

What is even more remarkable is that the same level of intellectual attainment is common to all. The first shall be last etc., and irrespective of education or intellect on Earth, in Heaven knowledge is a common currency distributed to all. And thanks to the common level of understanding the dissemination of recently acquired knowledge is no problem. Everyone understands everything instantly. This is another reason for the total lack of jealousy in Heaven.

Language

The principal modern language in Heaven is Tongues, which has been described as 'all things to all men'. There are certain exceptions to this general statement nevertheless. Small linguistic groups still exist where Tongues comes a poor second to the indigenous language. (In Trappist areas there is little evidence of any language at all, which gives rise to the derogatory phrase 'To shut one's trap'.)

Of these linguistic minorities the oldest and most widely spoken is Heavenese, from which much of modern Tongues is derived. Heavenese is similar in tone to the language of the King James translation of the Bible and employs similarly archaic phrasing. Since Heavenese is no longer the vernacular of contemporary Heaven we have only listed a few phrases here to assist the visitor in making himself or herself understood in the remoter areas of Heaven where it is still to be heard.

Heavenese	**Translation**
I pray that I may cross thy palm with silver …	How much?
I beg thine forgiveness …	Sorry, or tough
Ye, behold, yonder …	Watch it! Look at that over there
What speakest thou?	Pardon?
I pray deliverance unto ye chemists	How do I get to the chemists?
So is the Lord my guide, so shalt I not want …	Is it all right if we just look?
Verily, verily, verily …	Yes
Give me thine eyes, that I might see …	Please can I borrow your specs?
Naked I came into the world and naked I shall leave it …	I am a nudist
Is there anything thou wishest to make known unto me, my son?	Have you anything to declare?
Forgive me, for I have done thee wrong …	It's a fair cop!

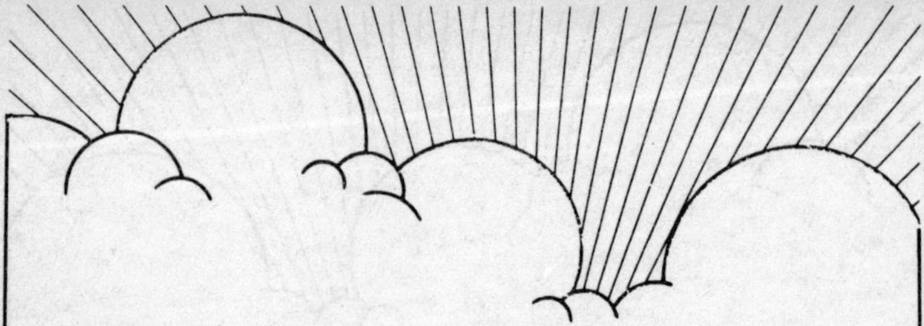

Heavenese	Translation
The sky was blue, and all that surrounded it was blue also	It's turned out nice again, hasn't it?
Forty days and forty nights have I fasted ...	Waiter, I am not happy with the service I am receiving
My vestments are indeed holy ...	My socks need darning
I see a place where I might rest	I'd like to rent one of your deck-chairs
I say unto thee, Nay ...	No
Shall I address thee with thy name?	What are you called?
It is written in the scriptures ...	It says here ...
Amen ...	That's all right with me, pal ...
I am the son of Luke, brother of Saul, grandson of the great Joshua, great great grandson of Samuel ...	I'm Kevin
It was spoken unto me by the Lord ...	A friend told me ...

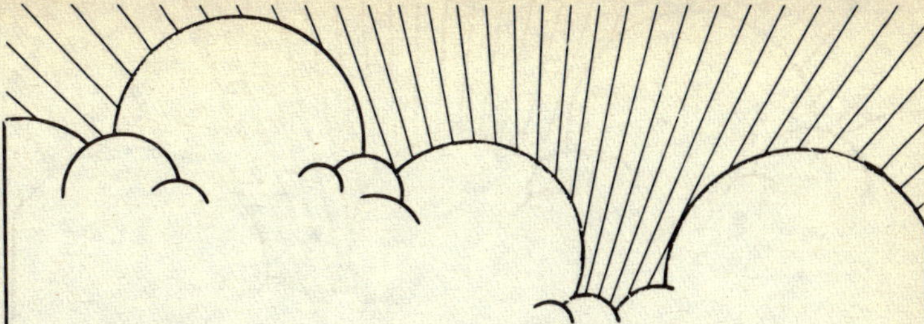

Heavenese	Translation
I pray that thou might show me the way ...	How do I get to ...?
I am filled with mystery and wonderment	Well, blow me!
Do any physicians reside therein?	Is there a doctor in the house?
The Lord is my Shepherd and he provideth me with good things ...	One shepherd's pie please
He gave unto me a son ...	I'm pregnant!
I have feasted on the fruits of my labours ...	I don't believe in saving (more commonly, 'Could you spare me a ...?)
And he saw that it was exceedingly good	He gave it the OK
He is all seeing and all doing	He is here, there and everywhere
You are not from these lands	Where are you from? (at times mistranslated as 'Home rule for Wales')

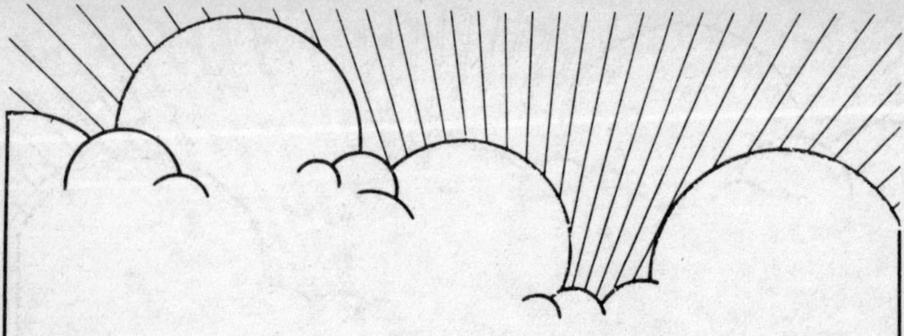

Heavenese	Translation
And the light will be seen to shine	Sunny periods with scattered isolated showers giving way to longer periods of sunshine later
I beseech thee with mine prayers	Ta!
Do not let thyself be bothered	Don't mention it
I did seek, and now have I found	I have been playing hide and seek – (often abbreviated to 'Boo!')
Art thou casting thine shackles upon me?	Want to make something of it?
I pray that I might feel refreshed	Where's the loo?
And so, it did come to pass …	Y'know …

Miracles

Heaven wouldn't be Heaven without miracles. Over 75 per cent of the visitors interviewed in a recent market research survey stated that they regarded their trip to Heaven as a 'bloody miracle'. Clearly miracles are what visitors expect and in spite of the insatiable demand none are ever disappointed. On average you can expect two or three sizeable miracles every day. And this excludes the dozens of minor miracles that take place without you even realising what has happened.

Ironically, a surfeit of miracles poses a threat to the unwary, a threat which takes two forms. The Miracle Index – the official scale which registers the national well being is of crucial importance to every soul in Heaven. A slight fall in this scale, no matter how minor can result in widespread panic praying. At times like this everyday life more or less grinds to a halt.

The second problem stems from this. This is the danger that arises from an acute awareness of anything that remotely resembles a miracle. So aware of the possibilities of miracles have resident souls become that the slightest deviation of events from their expected norm causes the automatic assumption that a miracle has taken place. In a few cases this has reached the scale of a clinical paranoia known as miraclemania. The symptoms are a constant preoccupation with events miraculous and divinely inspired. The victim becomes convinced that life is one long miracle, which to many, of course, it must seem after a life spent working for local government or the Department of Trade. This is an unfortunate disease since there is no miraculous cure for it. The only effective remedy discovered so far has been a sharp bang on the back of the head. This has usually brought the patient back to his senses and once again he can appreciate the difference between real miracles and apparent ones.

It is a nuisance for the would-be sightseer but unfortunately miracles can never be predicted. Naturally their sudden appearance adds to their mystery, but many have felt that much of their potential effectiveness is lost in this way. The Lord does not agree and for the time being we can rest assured that miracles will continue to crop up when we least expect them.

Traditional miracles like the wine-into-water and the loaves-and-fishes ones are now looked upon as being somewhat old-hat. Indeed some years ago there was a positive craze for turning water into wine and, less well known, back into water again. This swept across the Kingdom to such a degree that soon everyone was bored stiff with it and the idea has fallen from favour since then. Today the trend in miracles is towards the more exotic types of feat. Don't be at all surprised to find yourself temporarily turned into a frog (especially if you happened to be a Prince on Earth), or to wake up to find that your teeth have been turned to stone. You'll have no cause to worry: these are only temporary miracles that wear off after a couple of hours.

No discussion of miracles would be complete without a word about hospitals, for these are the places where the most astounding miracles occur. Hospitals in Heaven tend to be very small since no operations ever take place there and no one is ever required to stay the night. Every cure can be effected in a matter of seconds and, of course, very few people actually fall ill in Heaven.

Nudity

Since the unpleasantness in the Garden of Eden, nudity has been gradually declining in popularity. This isn't due to any Draconian clamp-down by the authorities; it's simply that knowledge has led most souls to accept the fact that it's easier to look pious and reverential when one is fully and decently clothed.

That's not to say that there aren't one or two brave souls who prance around without a stitch of clothing exclaiming, 'What was good enough for Paradise is good enough for Heaven,' but these exhibitionists are regarded with some disdain by the majority of those in Heaven, who are only too happy to have been clothed by the Lord. Apart from anything else it gets very chilly floating about on a cloud in the altogether.

Opera – the holy choir in vestibule

Music is an important part of life in Heaven and the Holy Choir in Vestibule have a justifiable universal reputation as being the leading choir in the heavens. They are the unofficial National Opera Company of Heaven.

The Choir's sole job is to entertain. They perform a mixed repertoire of works which are grouped under their Latin collective of *opera* (works). The Holy Choir in Vestibule sing everything and anything. Their versatility is unsurpassed being an amalgam of the Black and White Minstrels, The Osmonds, The King's Singers and the Red Army Choir, but inevitably success has brought with it several penalties. A demanding recording schedule has meant that the choir now performs few live recitals or concerts. This is only to be expected from a group of singers who are perpetually filling the top thirty places in the Heavenly top thirty charts.

Among their many great hits the following have been singled out for the highest Heavenly musical accolade, the Snow-white Disc Award:

- The Sound of the Holy Choir in Vestibule
- The Holy Choir in Vestibule Sings Reggae

- The Holy Choir in Vestibule – Abbey Road
- Songs for Swinging Saints (The Holy Choir in Vestibule)
- Golden Greats (The Holy Choir in Vestibule)
- The Holy Choir in Vestibule Live From The Holy Wood Bowl
- The Holy Choir in Vestibule In Confession
- The Holy Choir in Vestibule Sings Something Old, New, Hallowed and Blue
- The Holy Choir in Vestibule Go Punk
- HCV The Early Years
- Our Kind of Music (The Holy Choir in Vestibule)
- Messiah and The Holy Choir in Vestibule – Oratorios We Can Handel
- Matthew, John and The holy Choir in Vestibule – Passions
- The Holy Choir in Vestibule and Friends – Tidings (recorded live at the Shepherd's Benevolent Concert – Bethlehem in Judea)
- Singalongaholychoir

Although the choir as a whole rarely perform in public today, small sections are available for recitals at private functions and masonics. Their services are in great demand and early booking is strongly advised.

Pearly Gates, The

Numbered amongst the outstanding wonders of the universe; praised by poets from time immemorial, depicted in a thousand or more works of art from all corners of God's realm, the Pearly Gates are a truly stunning spectacle. Pearl E. Gates, the coloured architect after whom they were named, succeeded in capturing the spirit of the divine creator as no other designer before or since. The gates have been the supreme tourist attraction of Heaven from the day they were first hung and, like the Taj Mahal, the Eiffel Tower, the Humber Bridge and the Empire State Building, they seem to breathe the very life of the nation that inspired their erection.

The gates are a magnificent example of God's right hand at its best. Fashioned from wrought gold and encrusted with jasper and precious stones the gates soar to a majestic 98 feet at their highest point, towering above the time trodden path that leads to their very threshold. Here is omnipotence and a job well done. Visitors stand in bewilderment, passing angels turn in yet unbelieving wonder and even the Holy Spirit has been seen to stand in silence staring at the gates glinting in the golden light.

The symmetry is breathtaking, the artistry overpowering, the combined effect devastating. Were any single artefact to be singled out as a definitive expression of the supreme artist's work, there would be few who would question the election of these gates.

For all their majesty though there is piety in these holy portals. Looking at them for the first time it is easy to imagine the countless souls that have gazed on them with simple faith for longer than time can tell. In their radiant panels have been reflected the hopes and private fears of every generation since Creation itself. But edifices such as these do not exist without exacting their own price. And the price of the Pearly Gates is constant maintenance that grows more demanding each year. The chalices that adorn the upper reaches have to be taken down and sanctified every spring. A team of guilders work full-time attending to the damaged portions worn bare by the countless hands that have touched the lower parts of the gates in awe.

A more worrying aspect of the gates' maintenance has been the gradual sinking of the massive posts that support each one. These pillars of adamantine rock, imported specially from the Garden of Eden soon after it was opened to the public, have stood the test of time well enough – it is time that has not stood them, or to be precise the clouds of time in which they are sunk. The slow, but constant sinking of the pillars led to an alarming state of affairs several centuries ago when it was discovered that the gates could no longer be opened. Work started immediately to underpin the foundations and in the meantime the gates were closed. Since then all souls seeking admission have been obliged to enter Heaven by the small gate in the walls just to the left of the Pearly Gates themselves. Work is progressing well and the engineers in charge of the massive task are optimistic that the main gates will be opened before the Second Coming. Those who have witnessed the sight of the vast entrance being exposed as the gates swung open must count themselves among the truly fortunate. That sight will not be seen again in Heaven for many a long day.

For devotees of the unusual and bizarre the authorities have published several interesting statistics about the Pearly Gates, which we are pleased to reprint here with their kind permission:

1. The Gates of Heaven require the combined strength of 200 fit souls to open them.
2. The left-hand gate is the only one with a hallmark. The

right-hand gate has no such mark and as such is greatly inferior in trade-in value.

3. Five gallons of oil are needed to lubricate just one of the hinges on the Pearly Gates. There are two hinges on each gate.
4. To create the Pearly Gates on Earth you would need the total quantity of gold produced on Earth to date, as well as the estimated production for the next seventy-five years.
5. The scrap value of the Pearly Gates has been estimated to be £2,500,000,000,000,000,000,000,000,000,000,000 million.

(Regrettably photography is strictly forbidden in the vicinity of the Pearly Gates.)

Quick-fit exhausts
These are not available in Heaven.

Reverence
We hope that it goes without saying that visitors should try to display due reverence at all times in Heaven. The atmosphere is certainly conducive to this, thus making the task so much easier.

To those who have difficulty in adopting the correct posture the wisest course is to assume the stance and air of meek ineffectuality best exemplified by old-style Liberal Party candidates after they have lost their deposits. If you think reverence won't come naturally in your case, you may like to attend one of the excellent courses in 'Reverence and the world hereafter'. After long experience in imparting the appropriate techniques to willing souls, the Reverent Doctors (as the teachers are called) have managed to reduce the instruction period to a mere six weeks. It has to be admitted that in consequence many find the courses too demanding, especially as they are still busy getting acclimatised to Heaven itself.

As with blessing, the best policy to follow at first is not to question how and when to look reverential – 'Ours is not to reason why, ours is but to bless and sanctify' should be your motto. If you can look reverential for most of your time in Heaven, you won't go far wrong.

Moreover, just as blessing is an active state, so looking reverential is an essentially passive one. The two quite clearly can be, and are, interchangeable. Thus one can 'bless' one's cup of tea, or one can look reverentially at it. You can bless the stars, the moon and the light that shines forth, or you can gaze out at them with a pious glaze in your eyes. You can check your loose change with the air of a churchwarden casting an eye over the collection plate, or you can just bless it. In the majority of cases it doesn't matter which you choose provided you do one or the other.

A useful guide to reverence in Heaven is published by the authorities and is available at most booksellers. This is called *The Act of Reverence*. It is an outline of the rules and regulations governing reverence in every walk of Heavenly Life. As well as general reverence, the successful visitor to Heaven will want to indulge in certain specific acts of reverence. Giving up your seat in a cloud may be a blessed relief to you but it's an act of reverence to some other poor soul. Copying out the Bible in elegant italics as a gift to cheer up a friend who is feeling a bit down in the dumps is an act of reverence on a large scale. Though doing this a hundred times for the same reason is an act of monumental reverence bordering on the insane. Between these two extremes come a wide range of intermediate forms.

An act of reverence brings a peace of mind to whoever performs it. It's therefore difficult to determine who benefits most from it; the one who is revered or the one who does the revering. (This, incidentally, gives rise to the expression, 'I'll give you (a) peace of (my) mind.')

As a word of warning we should point out that it is an error, indeed a cardinal error to try to force too much reverence on unwilling recipients simply to improve your own peace of mind. Like miracle-making, reverence can become addictive, and nothing is worse than a pushy reverer. If you are going to act reverentially let it be unthinking. If you are in any doubts about your motives stay on the passive side and let others revere you.

Sin

Temptation

Temptation is of course an alien concept in Heaven. The only significant temptation that the visitor is likely to encounter is the desire to be more penitent than is really necessary. Negative, or inverted temptation is another matter, however.

In terms of Earthly pleasure inverted temptation is similar to the pay packet on the dogs. Temptation in terrestrial terms is usually a conflict between the will to act and the knowledge that to do so is wrong. Inverted temptation works in the opposite way. The result is that you become more and more adamant that you won't be tempted, and of course you never are. In the end you reach the stage at which you become so determined that you aren't going to eat that cream cake that other souls think that you've lost all reason and say that if you don't want that silly cake, they certainly do – and they eat it, so removing the source of your worry.

Universal Truths

There are two main truths:

Truth is universal, i.e. there is no lying. This is perfectly true (i.e. truthful). Everyone in Heaven tells the whole truth the whole time. To get by in Heaven visitors must follow the same policy. This is one of the Universal truths (see below).

Universal truths – These consist of a number of important truths, which have become more crucial to Heavenly existence over the years and have thereby taken on the character of laws, though no one can actually be arrested for breaking them. Clearly it's truthful to say that your name is Roger, if indeed it is Roger, but this isn't exactly the truth that's going to shake the world. No, the truths in this category deal with weightier issues such as honesty, love, understanding and humility. The corner stone of all universal truths is the one commandment 'Thou shalt not'. This is the succinct version of the Ten Commandments delivered to Moses.

As has been the case with so many traditional aspects of life in Heaven, universal truths have not escaped the inroads of progressive thinking and commercialisation. Looking around the streets of Heaven you will find many examples of universal truths expressed in blatantly contemporary terms: 'It's great to be pious', 'Be an A.M. Thanksgiver', 'Snogging is Right Out' – these are just a few of many dozens of similar appeals to the youth of Heaven to accept the ancient mantle of truth and piety.

Vestments, Holy

Folk in Heaven always appear similarly clad – not as God originally intended us to be (that idea is as old as Eve), but decently garbed in what have become generally termed Holy Vestments. (Underwear is referred to as Holy Stringed Vestments.)

Holy Vestments may lack something of the rich colour and varied gaiety of other forms of traditional costume, but they have the merit of being eminently practical. Holy Vestments are loose, white and shapeless. In a society where everyone is equal the authorities are at pains to cover up earthly physical forms which might otherwise distract or embarrass passers-by.

Wearing such garments takes a little getting used to and would-be visitors to Heaven may like to get into the

Heaven habit by wearing an old sheet, with a hole cut out of it, on Earth.

Holy Vestments should be worn with the label on the inside. This may sound obvious, but it is surprising how many souls dash out of the house only to discover that they are wearing their vestments inside out. Worse still many of them panic and in a vain bid to turn the vestment the right way round while still maintaining some sense of modesty end up almost throttling themselves.

Holy Vestments are unisex and choice is deliberately kept to the minimum. Those requiring larger vestments 'for the fuller soul' either have to order in advance, or else buy two smaller sizes and stitch them together. The only concession made to sartorial refinement is an optional layer of insulation. This is particularly useful for those who intend to spend any length of time sitting on a cloud.

Heavenly footwear is equally unadventurous. Like it or not, rope sandals are all that you will be offered. These are traditionally worn without socks and anyone seen wearing even the soberest pair of socks is usually marked out as a rebel or an eccentric. It's a wise precaution to insist on a test walk before you make your purchase. Sandal purveyors will expect you to make such a request and by law they are obliged to let you try out your sandals for a fourteen day period, during which you are entitled to a full refund if you are not entirely satisfied with what they have given you. In spite of rigid controls a number of cheaper types of rope sandal have been imported and sold on the Heavenly market. These do not last anything like as long as the traditional home manufactured ones. Since they cannot be distinguished from each other there has been a growth in the number of 'sandal-bars' in recent years. These specialise in fast, efficient re-roping. The best we came across was the Achilles Heel Bar.

The young souls of Heaven have not been short of ideas for livening up their footwear, but none of the many chiro-crazes has lasted for long. Stiletto-heeled Sandals, Winkle-Picker Sandals, Bovver Rope Sandals, all have come and gone. The only one to have made any headway is the St Martin's air-wear sandal which is still popular among a coarser section of the Heavenly fraternity. Rope sandal wellingtons and slippers are also popular for the aquatically inclined.

One further word of warning with regard to all holy vestments is that each article carries the wording 'Property of the Kingdom of Heaven – Do Not Remove'. Under no circumstances should you try to take any of these with you, should you leave Heaven for any reason. It's unlikely that you will be tempted in this way, but we would be failing in our duty if we did not make this point clear.

(*Note:* People in jeans, motor-cycle gear and heavily soiled work clothes will not be allowed admittance to the kingdom of heaven. By order of the management.)

Who's Who in Heaven

God Born: (Craven): time immemorial. Ruler of Earth and the Universe. Sage/Prophet/Counsel to Mankind/Creator of all. **Other names:** 'The Way', 'The Truth', 'The Light', 'The Almighty', 'The Lord', 'The Maker', 'Father' etc. **Educated:** by himself. **Interests:** healing/blessing/loving/cherishing/worshipping/being humble/forgiving/golf. **Publications:** *The Holy Bible* (Old Testament), *The Holy Bible* (New Testament). **Family:** One son/Mankind.

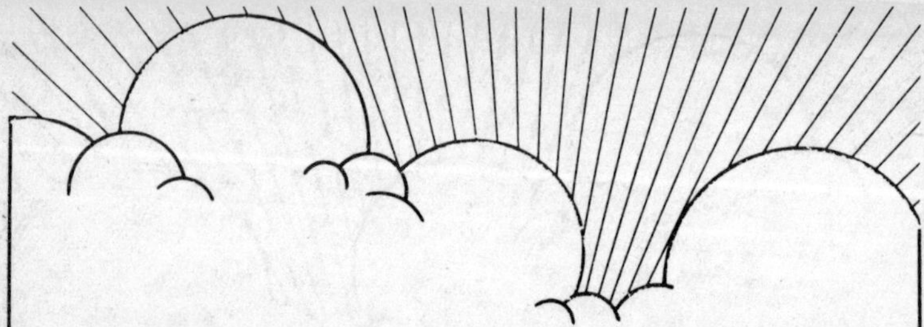

St Peter Born 37BC. Keeper of the Gate of Heaven (Pearly Gates registered keyholder). **Other names:** 'The Rock', 'Rocky'. **Educated:** Nazareth High and University of Jerusalem Institute of Science, Technology and Discipling. **Interests:** repenting/giving thanks/saying sorry/fishing. **Publications:** *The Holy Bible* (in conjunction with others), *St Peter's Book of the Heavenly Countryside – A Thousand Years Out In Heaven, Pete, Matt, Mark, Luke Fall Into Adventure* (autobiography), *The Gospel According to St Peter Giant Colouring Book, The Disciple Handbook.* **Family:** Unmarried.

Satan Born 7.1.1. Self-appointed leader and vociferous champion of sinners everywhere. **Other names:** 'Lucifer', 'The Devil', 'Derek'. **Educated:** Not at all. **Interests:** Sinning/More sinning/Even more sinning/General nastiness/Undoing good works/Making it rain when it's not wanted/Giving people colds/Ruining marriages/Inciting others to undo good works/Violence/Foul deeds/Evil thoughts. **Publications:** *The Devil's Sunbird Calendar* (from now until Doomsday), *For your Sins, The Good Feud Guide, I was a Teenage Werewolf* (autobiography). **Family:** Divorced 9,000,000,000 times; all his children are bastards.

Sir Galahad Born AD 1421. Very, very good knight with lots of qualities to recommend him. Reputed to have the best breath in the universe. **Other names:** 'The Bold One', 'The Brave One', 'The Chivalrous One', 'The One Who Doesn't Interfere with Women', 'Nancy Boy', 'Kenny'. **Educated:** King Arthur's School, Camelot. **Interests:** Saving damsels in distress/Performing acts of great self-denial/Acting the good knight/Round Table activities.

Publications: *The Celebates Kama Sutra*. **Family:** None, unmarried.

Florence Nightingale Born 1820. English nurse noted for her good works during the Crimean War, now Minister of Health for the Kingdom of Heaven. **Interests:** Healing/Tending the sick/Applying bandages/Cleaning out perforated ulcers/Treating gastric complaints/Caring for pet owls. **Publications:** *How To Make The Most of Your body, How To Make The Most of Someone Else's Body, The Illustrated Book of the Tourniquet* (colour), *Do-it-yourself Home Surgery* (with stain proof cover). **Family:** None.

John the Baptist Born 35 BC. Baptiser and preacher. **Other names:** 'Zacharias's Son', 'Sach's Lad', 'Johnnie', 'Uncle John'. **Educated:** to CSE level. **Interests:** Preaching/Baptising/Wind Surfing/All other water sports. **Publications:** *The Wind Surfer's Handbook, Tails You Lose* (autobiography). **Family:** Not yet married.

Adam Born 6.1.1. First inhabitant of the Garden of Eden. First man ever to taste the forbidden fruit. Now owner of a grocery chain in Heaven. Normal looking, hence expression 'I wouldn't know him from Adam'. **Other names:** 'Mr Hendricks'. **Interests:** Anything to do with fig leaves. **Family:** Divorced.

X-Tras and Rewards

No one talks of wages in Heaven. Remuneration takes the form of what are euphemistically called Fruits of Labour. These are more than pure wages. They are more too than a straightforward salary. They encompass a wide range of benefits which everyone receives without question. There are company (Heavenly company) clouds, manna vouchers, Angelic Express Cards as well as generous bonuses and long holidays.

None of these is open to negotiation. They have to be accepted, even if at times they appear to be absurdly generous. Furthermore, the value of Fruits of Labour, which are very crudely the average national earnings, more than keep pace with inflation. They increase each year, but inflation remains static at nought per cent.

While it can be argued that X-tras and rewards like these blunt initiative and competition, they do lead to the most equal society in the universe, and we're bound to say, one with the fewest economic problems.

You

The time has come for us to ask you to reflect for a moment on the other crucial factor in the Heavenly equation – YOU!

As our guide book draws to a close and as the wonders of the world beyond the grave lie spread before you, stop for a moment. Put aside starry-eyed dreams of immortality and days of unending sunshine and ask yourself two questions: 'Do I believe in Heaven?' 'Do I believe in myself?'

These need not tie you up in helpless strands of metaphysics. Only an honest, down-to-Earth answer is required. God is listening remember, and he knows your answers already – but he'd like to hear you put them across in your own way.

ZACCHARUS	see below
ZADOK	see below
ZAREPHAT	see below
ZEALOTS	see below
ZEBEDEE	see below
ZEBOIM	see below
ZEBULUM	see below
ZECHARIAH	see below
ZEDEKIAH	see below
ZEPHANIAH	see below
ZERUBBABEL	see below
ZIKLAG	see below
ZILPAH	see below
ZIMRI	see below
ZIN	see below
ZION	see below
ZIPH	see below
ZIPPORAH	see below
ZOAN	see below
ZOAR	see below
ZOBAH	see below
ZOPHAR	see below

(see Bible for full details)

OTHER GUIDE BOOKS IN THE SAME SERIES

Abraham's Bosom and its Environs
The Eternal Home
Eden Garden Suburb
Isle of The Blest, The
Elysian Fields, Home of the meek and mild
Valhalla-upon-Avon
NW Paradise
SW Paradise
NE Paradise
Central Paradise
The Celestial Riviera
The Pearly Gates
Costa Heaven

Out Of Print

Hell
Hell and Damnation
Hell, Damnation and the Lands Sloth

Each guide book provides an attractive and authoritative look at the land, the country, and the people. Hard, or limp bound, they're bound to help you on your way through the hereafter. Available through all good bookshops, travel agents, newsagents and department stores or direct from:

KINGDOM OF HEAVEN TOURIST AUTHORITY
LORD'S WAY
HEAVEN WC1.

HOLIDAY READING

Don't forget to take a book! These and countless other never-to-be-remaindered titles are available free from the Notionwide Book Club, P.O. Box $33\frac{1}{3}$, Heaven S.W.17.

Country Diary of An Edwardian Prophet
Teach Yourself Blessing
The Readers Digest Book Of The Miracle
Who-Was-Who
Do-It-Yourself Penitence
Do-It-Yourself Sinning
Wish you Hadn't Done-It-Yourself Repentance
It Shouldn't Happen To An Angel
Paradise Found
God – His Own Story
Bible Two!
The Sensuous Saint
Disciples In Their Underpants
The Halo Owners' Handbook
Hell on £5 a Day
Brewers Dictionary of Cain & Abel
The Good Lord Guide

HOTELS

The Holy Day Inn 630 rooms (all with c & h, t.v., prayer mat etc.) 3 bars. Parking for 250 clouds. Open all year.

The Heaven Hilton We like to think that when you stay with us you stay for a reason. And that reason is quality. The Heaven Hilton offers you unrivalled excellence in a contemplative setting. Plenty of space for meditation and seeking thine inner being.

Inn On The Ark For a warm friendly welcome you can't beat the Inn On The Ark. 'We're small, we're clean ... and we haven't forgotten the meaning of hospitality.' (Animals always welcome.) Proprietor, Mr Noah.

St John The Baptist For a night, a week-end, a week, a month ... The St John The Baptist can offer you 'The Word' in comfort. Our spa water is reknowned the world over and the Salome Suite the perfect setting for your Heavenly honeymoon.

The Excelsior (part of the 'Trust Ye' House Group) 2,000 rooms (each with own swimming pool). Conference facilities.

The Lord's Head Mine staff will thee comfort in every possible way. R. Lord-Almighty (Proprietor).

Sinners Arms Closed for repentance.

Ecumenical View Only three minutes from the Gates of Heaven. Small, clean, friendly, with unbeatable view from the roof top where you can see over 4,300 churches. Proprietress, Miss Tickle.

Hotel Presbyterian (Temperance) Low rates, good food. Ideal for penitence, sufferance, chastity. Ask for our special Piety-break terms. Stay one night and you can stay the next 340 free!

Ma Ramsbottom's B & B. Vacancies all year round. Tariff on request (No Lepers).

The Tri-Umvirate (Part of The Three-In-One Chain of Motels.) Convenient for the cloud. Fully Air Conditioned.

Heavenly Pastures Unrivalled chance to enjoy a complete life of un-uproarious living. (No c & h, no t.v., no carpets, no bed in all rooms.) Restaurant sits 1 (and its permanently closed anyway). 41 miles from the town centre.

Grand Hotel We are quite simply the best hotel in Heaven. Comfort and facilities second to none. English, French and Kosher cuisine. Special facilities for the disabled and neighbours' asses. 900 rooms. One stable block.

Room At The Inn (no vacancies)

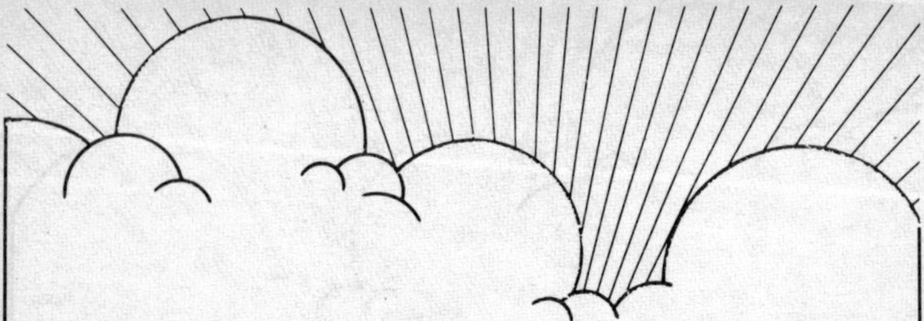

EATING OUT

Manna 'n Chips is the bright new fast-food store in the centre of Heaven. And we mean fast! Before the service – after the service – anytime! Let us feed you now and evermore!

Loaves and Fishes Our small, seafood restaurant has room for a surprising 5,000 diners. And it's regularly packed – why? Because we use only the finest bread from Heaven and fill it with the tastiest, chunkiest, crispiest cod you're ever likely to put your lips around. It's the next best thing to sinning!

Venus de Milo Arms Traditional English pub grub at reasonable prices. And in Heavenly surroundings. That's what's on offer today – and everyday. What could be better? 'Worth a Visit' – Michel Inn Guide.

Deuteronomy's Chop House When you need filling we'll fill the bill. Our range of steaks (house speciality St Laurence) is the widest in town. Everyday – noon till late. (Sorry no pilgrims without a tie.)

Chez Leviticus Late nite cafe/diner. While away those repentative hours over a bottle of holy water in our select cellars. (Sinners night – Tuesday.)

First Supper You're never alone when you bite into a 'First Supper Burger'. Fresh outa the oven – just like Jesus used to make 'em! Eat In – Take Out – The brightest taste around.

Gentilles (formally Lentiles) Simply the best in Kosher cooking, already. Wine and Dine to the music of regular artistes – 'The Chosen Few'. English menu on request.

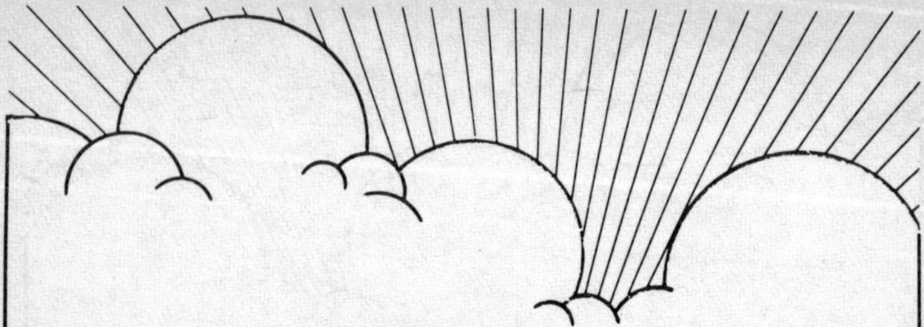

ENTERTAINMENT

Shrines Pray, worship, ordain ... in the vaults of the liveliest night club in town (Host – Dicky Shrine).

Walls of Babylon 'Mecca of Heaven'. We're large, we're friendly, and we're just waiting for you to come and enjoy our unique form of entertainment. Dancing nightly – closed Sabbath.

Valhalla For the best in Soul music.

The Wheel Tappers and Blasphemers Club Sorry, closed indefinitely.

Lilliput – God's Little World. Paradise's very own miniature village. It was lost to those on earth – but now you can find it once again, right bang in the heart of God's kingdom. A miniature world of enchantment. Includes model railway.

Creation World See the story of the world you've just left behind unfurled before your very eyes. The story of the Creation as you've never seen it before. Performance lasts about six days so do bring something warm to wear and plenty of food. Café and gift shop.

Bible Land A funfair park with tons of good, clean entertainment for all the family. On similar lines to Disney Land – only not quite as good. Try to catch the Holy Ghost train ... it'll send a shiver down your ecumenical robes.

CLASSIFIED ADVERTISEMENTS

Miniclouds Station, airport etc. ... Miniclouds offer a fast, reliable taxi service to all parts of Heaven. Clean, efficient, economic. Miniclouds are at your service 24-hours a day. Miniclouds – Heaven, anywhere, anytime.

Tense, nervous headache? Take **The Bible**! Read **The Bible** morning, noon and night to relieve tense, nervous headaches, depression, anxiety and manifold other ailments. Available in small, medium and King James sizes.

OLD HALOES – We buy old haloes for cash – any make, any condition. Halo Breaker's Ltd, Railway Sidings, Heaven, E.2.

Penitence arranged, repentance accepted, forgiveness when you want it – all these and much, much more available when you join the Christian Church. Branches throughout the Kingdom of Heaven and overseas.

WONDROUS THINGS – for all your fashion problems. This is the boutique with the very latest in shrouds and vestments. All leading names stocked including: **Man of the Cloth**, **Man at C. of E.**, **Trappist Girl**, **Ex-communication cords** and **Bless-U Jeans**.

The Lord works in mysterious ways and every year it costs him more. Please give generously to – The Lord's Works Appeal Fund, P.O. Box 101, Heaven, E.C.4.

This year learn how to resist temptation the fast, efficient

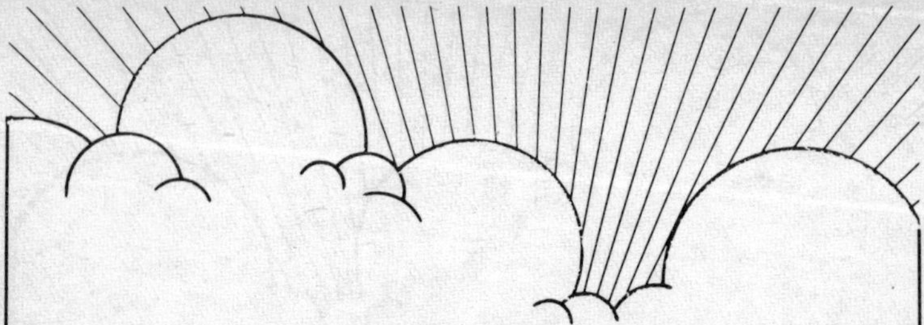

way at the Swedish Sauna and Massage Parlour. Our 81-year course will enable you to resist temptations you never even knew existed. Every conceivable vice (and a few inconceivable ones) are catered for. We are leading experts in temptation. Now we'll teach you to resist it too. The Swedish Sauna and Massage Parlour, Rue de Awakening, Heaven, S.W.10.

MANNA FROM HEAVEN – For all your catering problems, hot cross buns, and unleavened bread choose Manna from Heaven on any main street. (Parties and Masonics catered for.)

The Lord is my Shepherd – who is yours? Trouble controlling your flock? Then ask the Lord for details. Just get down on your knees and pray. 24-hour answering service.

Amaze your friends: turn water into wine; part the waters; make bushes explode ... and hundreds more tricks from The Miracle Joke Shop, P.O. Box 13, Heaven, N.7.

ANGLING Amazing new results using the **Cast Thine Nets** method. With chapters on Sea Fishing, Coarse Fishing, Game Fishing, you too can become a fisher of men. Write to The Holy Bible (Publ.) Ltd, 133 Holy Way, Heaven, W.C.3.

Relax in an Ass's Milk Bath – the modern effective way to relax away those tensions and worries. Ass's Milk Baths are available in sachets, tubes, half-gallon bottles, or direct from the ass itself.

Tea, just like mum used to make it. Old Ma Deuteronomy's Olde English Tea Shoppe. Teas, snacks, light meals, Evangelists always welcome.

Burnt Offerings? You needn't any more – with a 'Joan of Arc'. Just clip it onto your offering and avoid embarrassing burns in future. No need for costly wiring or re-plumbing. Lasts up to 10,000 years.

Ex-prophet offers discreet, personal advice on all matters of the mind and body. Available for home consultation. Hundreds of validated testimonies. Also available for weather forecasts and pools forecasts. St Craig, P.O. Box 147, Heaven, N.W.5.

FAST PRAY Today hundreds of people are being held back in their jobs because of poor, or slow, praying. But now it can be cured. Thanks to our amazing course in speed-praying. We promise to improve your praying in 6 weeks ... or your money back. Fast Pray, P.O. Box 12, Heaven, W.C.2.

Vestal Virgins available now – ring us and tell us your requirements. Vestal Virgin Hire. Branches throughout Heaven.

Computaprophecy The clean, effective way to foresee all your own ends. Write yesterday for details. Computaprophecy, St Abbingdon Road, Heaven, E.4.

The God Food Guide A guide to eating out in Heaven with recommendations of food to sav(i)our. Also **The God**

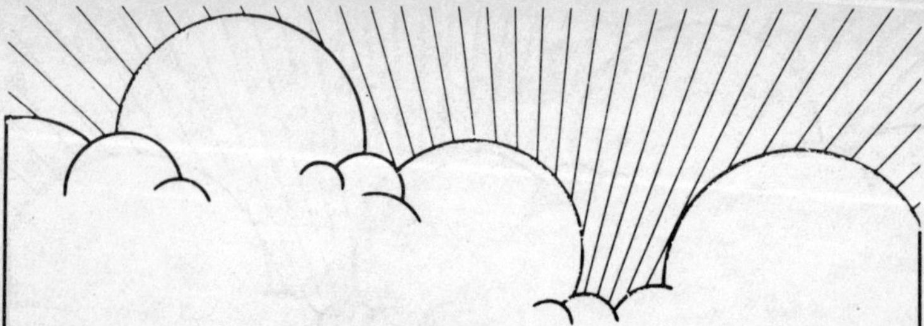

Pub Guide and **The God Snack Guide**. The Holy Bible (Publ.) Ltd. Available through all god bookshops.

THE SOUND OF SILENCE Amazing new double-album featuring 75 minutes of some of the all time golden greats in silent prayer. Available only through SPCK Records Ltd. Price 3 rosaries and a hail Mary (+ VAT).

SERVICES

Forgivefulness Need forgiving? Come to us – we're the experts! 'FORGIVE 'N FORGET' – the fastest forgiving service in town. (If you'll forgive us for saying so.) Leave your sins with us by 10.00 and we'll have forgiven you for them by 6.00. None better.

Ghosts Ghosts required for interesting and varied work. Must be prepared to travel and to work nights. Good pay and conditions. All enquiries to O. Cromwell, P.O. Box 13, Heaven, S.E.2.

Immortal-Invisible The fast new way to get rid of spots and stains. Immortal-Invisible – just rub it on and wipe it off. And see the difference. Better than washing. Available from all hardware stores.

Bless This House The simple way to buy and sell your house. Bless This House offers unrivalled expertise in property transactions. Buying, selling ... or just consecrating your home ... give us a call.

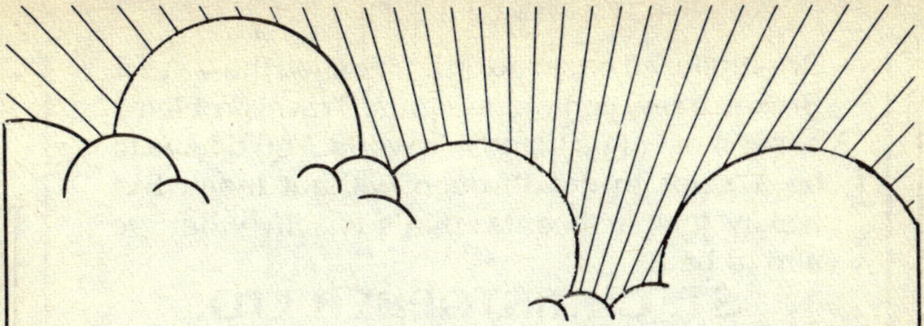

A Life of Devotion After the life before you'll wish you'd had one. But it's still not too late. Start repenting today.

Poltergeist Removals We've been moving things for over 2,000 years. Let us help you when you want to move. You'll find us in the Holy Pages.

Clip-on-wings Makes you look and feel like an angel. Without going to the trouble of being Angelic. Just one of a whole range of accessories. Available through Reward in Heaven (Toys, Gifts & Fancy Goods).

Lost Souls Found The Heaven Detective Agency

Amen! The last word in deodorant – for men! (From Heaven Scent – the makers of Hai Church.)

Having a Halo Installed? It needn't cost as much as you think. Especially if you have it installed now. Halo & Son Ltd. (Member of the association of Halo Installers), P.O. Box 89, Heaven, N.6.

It's a good life in the Angels – water-skiing, skin diving, scuba diving, it's all there – and much, much more! Come and have a chat and a prayer with us, and see if we can't convert you. The Angels – The Professionals!

Unwanted prayers needed urgently for people on Earth. Please send your unwanted prayers to The Prayers for Earth Appeal, Blue St Peter, Heaven, W.1.

Breathalysed once too often? Fiddled the V.A.T.? Broken a few commandments? Travel problems beset most of us in today's world. You'd have to be a saint to get through without them. But luckily for our clients, that's exactly what we aim to be at . . .

ST. CHRISTOPHER LTD. (TRAVEL ORGANIZERS)

Contact us with your travel problems — the independent traveller is our speciality.

ST. CHRISTOPHER LTD.
81 VALLEY OF THE SHADOWS BOULEVARD,
HEAVEN W.8. (Part of the St. Thomas of Cook Group)

Reincarnation's chilling finger beckons when you least expect it. Snatched from the other world, the unsuspecting can be transformed into a mouse, a toad, a tax inspector, a rat . . . or worse. Every year thousands of souls disappear in this way. Forgotten by the Heavenly host at large, they pass their terrestial days, changed beyond redemption in the form of some poor animal or other godforsaken creature. It can be a terrible experience. Now, at last, there is a fund to support those who have lost a loved-one through reincarnation.

THE REINCARNATION BENEVOLENT FUND exists to help those in distress.

Please send contributions however small, to:
THE REINCARNATION BENEVOLENT FUND,
42 PLAZA OF THE SAINTS,
HEAVEN S.W.1.

Reincarnation - it could happen to you . . .

PEOPLE BECOME PAIN IN THE HALO?

SODOM!!!

Yes, why not arrange that special package tour for the person of your choice. Pack them off to the historic city of Sodom (twin town Milton Keynes). Full details of our special non- return holidays from:

Visitors Committee, Get Stuffed St.,
Sodom, Hell E.6.

SPIRIT WILLING - FLESH WEAK?
WITH THIS UNIQUE POLICY
SALVATION IS ON CALL ANYTIME!

MEDICICOVER is your insurance against sin. It's your personal guarantee that a fully qualified redeemer is on hand day and night, seven days a week, fifty-two weeks a year waiting to answer your call whenever sin has struck.

For as little as three Hail Mary's a day, MEDICICOVER protects you, your family, and even friends, relatives, au pairs and attractive young models who just happen to be around when sin strikes.

MEDICICOVER doesn't change your relationship with the Lord and Maker, but it does give you the blessed peace of mind that comes from knowing that you'll get instant forgiveness anytime you call.

For full details complete the attached coupon.
Be honest with yourself and post it right now.

NAME..
ADDRESS..
....*TEL*

ETERNITY IS A LONG TIME

ENJOY IT TO THE FULL WITH

The Pilgrimage Discount Card is the ideal way to make the most of Heaven without paying the Earth! It opens the doors of all Heaven's high spots for the lowest rates. Send away for yours today to:

The Pilgrimage Discount Scheme,
Heavenly Travel Service,
Revelation 25,
Heaven W8

PERSPECTIVE — WE ALL NEED IT

If you're happy, or contented, why not speak to someone who couldn't give a tinker's cuss.

Telephones countrywide **unmanned night & day**

THE PHARISEES

And we can do without your help too, so don't bother to write to:

The Honorary Secretary,
The Pharisees,
13 What's-it-to-you Road,
Heaven N.W.4